Contents

Executive Summary

The long tradition of local control over K–12 education has distinct benefits: it promotes civic engagement and local involvement in education, and it can make spending more efficient. Meaningful local control, however, requires at least some of the funding for education to come from local sources. The property tax is a good local revenue source with distinct advantages over its alternatives, local sales and income taxes. In practice, the property tax plays a central role in funding K–12 education in the United States, accounting for 36 percent of total revenue.

Nationwide, 36 percent of funding for K–12 public schools comes from local property taxes on homes, businesses, farms, and land. *Source: Alex Potemkin/ Getty Images/iStock Unreleased*

But the local property tax is not perfect. One frequent criticism is that property-wealthy school districts can raise a lot more money than districts with smaller property tax bases. State aid can compensate for that inequity, but even well-designed state funding might not be sufficient for the poorest school districts to provide their students the requisite adequate education, let alone a high-quality one. Also, the heavier the reliance on state aid, the larger the risk of funding cuts during recessions, when the major sources of state government tax revenue—sales and income taxes—are likely to decline.

The two major sources of funding for public education—local property taxes and state aid—have weaknesses as well as strengths. There is no easy choice between these two forms of financing K–12 education.

Herein lies the dilemma: The two major sources of funding for public education—local property taxes and state aid—have weaknesses as well as strengths. There is no easy choice between these two forms of financing K–12 education. The property tax–school funding dilemma is about overcoming the shortcomings of both major funding sources while ensuring that school funding systems can finance an adequate education for all students equitably and efficiently.

Chapter 1 briefly reviews school funding in the United States; chapter 2 describes the property tax and steps that some states have taken to improve its fairness and efficiency. Chapter 3, which focuses on state aid, is a primer on crafting a high-quality state-aid program and reviews the formulas states use to allocate aid. Chapter 4 describes how the property tax–school funding dilemma has played out in five states:

California, Massachusetts, South Carolina, Texas, and Wisconsin. Chapter 5 evaluates the property tax and state-aid systems in the five case study states.

This evaluation then informs the policy recommendations, presented in detail in chapter 6:

- States should use a mix of local property tax revenue and state aid to provide their students a high-quality education. In particular, states must resist calls to stop using local property taxes to fund schools.

- States should improve their property tax systems. Improving the equity and efficiency of the property tax is likely to increase its acceptance as an important component in financing public education.

- States should allocate aid to local school districts in a manner that ensures all students can receive a high-quality education. Systems of state school aid should be based on a formula that accounts for school districts' differing costs of providing all students an adequate education.

- To prevent cuts in state education aid during recessions, states need sufficient rainy-day funds to draw upon when state tax revenues decline.

- The federal government should provide additional funding to lower-income states that lack revenue to provide their students an adequate education. The federal government should also consider granting additional aid to local school districts to remedy learning losses arising from the COVID-19 pandemic.

CHAPTER 1
Introduction

Property taxation and school funding are closely linked in the United States. Nearly half the total revenue supporting public elementary and secondary education comes from local governments, and 80 percent of the local share comes from property taxes. Viewed from the opposite perspective, more than half of total property taxes in the United States pay for public K–12 education.

Electing local school board members, such as in the Los Angeles Unified School District, is one way taxpayers exercise control over school district decisions.
Source: SEIU Local 99/flickr

This chapter presents some basic statistics about K–12 education revenues, with an emphasis on the property tax. After discussing local control of education revenue and spending and the virtues of the property tax, we introduce the two major goals of a school finance system—equity and adequacy—and explain how these goals have been defined. We conclude with an explanation of the property tax–school funding dilemma.

The Importance of Property Taxes for Funding Schools

In school year 2018–2019, public education revenue in the United States totaled $771 billion. As figure 1.1 shows, nearly half (47 percent) came from state governments, slightly less than half (45 percent) from local government sources, and a modest share from the federal government (8 percent). The figure shows that 36 percent of public K–12 revenue came from property taxes. The remaining portion of local

government revenue (about 9 percent of total revenue) was generated by other local taxes; fees and charges for things like school lunches and athletic events; and contributions from individuals, organizations, or businesses.

Figure 1.2 shows changes in the local, state, and federal shares of funding for K–12 education over the last century, and several trends stand out. The federal share of funding has never been very large, exceeding 10 percent only from 2009 through 2011, when the American Recovery and Reinvestment Act delivered extra funding as part of the stimulus package during the Great Recession. (These data do not extend to a second temporary increase in federal funding during the COVID-19 pandemic.) In school year 1919–1920, the local share was more than 80 percent and state share less than 20 percent. Between then and 1950, the state's share of public school funding rose to 40 percent. During the 1970s, largely influenced by the *Serrano v. Priest* series of school funding court cases in California, the state government share of school funding rose to 47 percent. Since then, with the exception of two years, the state share has remained between 45 and 50 percent of total public education revenues.

Figure 1.3 tracks the contribution of the local property tax to K–12 funding beginning in school year 1988–1989. As the figure shows, the role of the local property tax in financing public education in the United States has remained remarkably stable in the decades since 1989. In 1988–1989, the property tax contributed 35.8 percent of total K–12 funding, and it contributed 36.2 percent of total funding in 2018–2019. The ups and downs in figure 1.3 relate to business cycles; specifically, when the economy heads into a recession, K–12 education depends more on the local property tax, and after the recession, that reliance eventually falls.

Figure 1.1

K–12 Public Education Revenue by Source, United States, 2018–2019

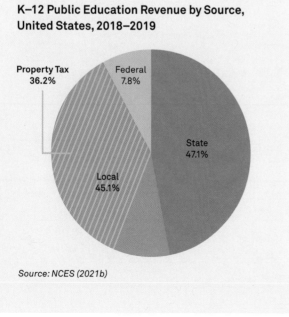

Source: NCES (2021b)

Figure 1.2

K–12 Public Education Revenue by Level of Government

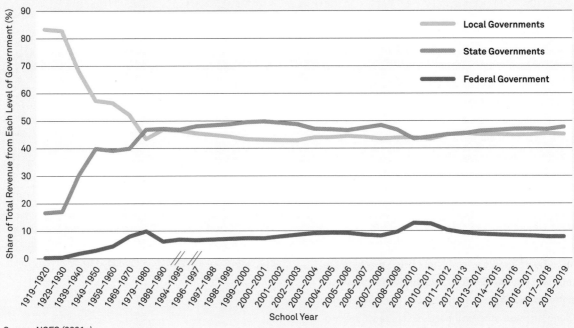

Source: NCES (2021a)

Figure 1.3

Property Tax Revenue as a Percentage of Total K–12 Education Revenue

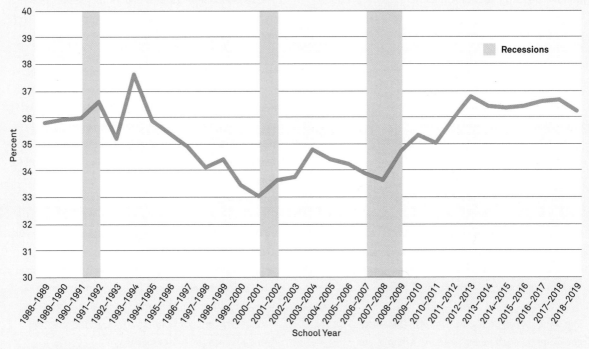

Source: NCES (2021b)

Local Control

Although Americans have a long history of distrusting the federal government, a large majority have confidence in local governments. In a 2019 Gallup poll, 71 percent of respondents said they had either a fair amount or a great deal of trust in their local governments' ability to handle local problems. The same poll found that only 51 percent expressed similar confidence in the federal government and 63 percent in their state government. School districts are one of the most important types of U.S. local government.

In the United States, local control of schools is popular. Taxpayers, parents among them, have a say in how schools are run, how much teachers are paid, what courses are offered, and what physical facilities are needed. Local control can make school spending more efficient, because home values are strongly influenced by the quality of a community's schools. A home constitutes a substantial portion of many people's net worth. Thus, homeowners are motivated to pay attention to their community's school funding—to approve worthwhile spending and oppose wasteful spending (Fischel 2001). If school spending was totally funded by state dollars, residents would have less incentive to closely monitor their schools. For background on how court decisions have influenced school funding systems in the United States, see Odden and Picus (2020) and Kenyon, Munteanu, and Paquin (2023).

Virtues of the Property Tax

For local control to be meaningful, residents must be able to decide, either directly or through elected school boards, how much to spend each year on education. How should this money be raised? In many ways, the property tax is an ideal local tax for funding public education.

The benefits residents receive from their local government, such as high-quality schools, are

Independent and Dependent School Districts

The more than 90,000 local governments in the United States include 12,754 independent school districts, which have substantial autonomy and can impose and collect taxes. Some school districts (1,307) are dependent governments, which means that they are agencies of other state, county, municipal, or township governments, and they receive revenue from their parent government (U.S. Census Bureau 2019).

Thirty states have only independent school districts, and four states (Alaska, Hawaii, Maryland, and North Carolina) and the District of Columbia have only dependent school districts. Sixteen states have some combination of independent and dependent school districts.

generally manifested in higher property values. In a well-structured property tax system, without complex or confusing property tax limitations, the tax is both visible and transparent. Voters considering an expenditure, such as building a new elementary school or hiring additional teachers, will have clear information on both the benefits and the costs to expect. Projected costs are the extra property tax payments needed to finance the new expenditures. In many circumstances, then, property taxes reflect the price residents pay for local government services.

The property tax base (that is, the assessed value of all property within a jurisdiction) is also an appropriate source for local tax revenue because the tax base is immobile. As Langley and Youngman (2021) noted,

Because land is completely immovable, local voters can choose a package of taxes and services without concern that small tax differentials with neighboring jurisdictions could drive away this portion of the tax base. Buildings are a long-term investment, slow to respond to small tax advantages or disadvantages.

Texas has over a thousand independent school districts, more than any other state, and educates 11 percent of all public school students in the nation, including these students at Park Crest Middle School in Pflugerville Independent School District. *Source: Bob Daemmrich/Alamy Stock Photo*

In contrast, shoppers can easily avoid a local sales tax by driving a few miles, and businesses can avoid local income taxes by relocating office headquarters.

Compared with revenues from sales and income taxes, those from the property tax vary less over business cycles: the property tax base is more stable over time than income or taxable sales, and local property tax rates are also usually adjusted annually to offset changes in the market value of property, whereas changes in local sales and income tax rates are difficult to enact and infrequent (Kenyon and Munteanu 2021).

School Funding Equity and Adequacy

Fairness is an inherently normative concept. For at least a century, discussions of fairness in public school funding have centered on inequalities in school spending and revenues. For the last several decades, debates about fairness in school funding have emphasized providing all students an adequate education.

Over time and across the nation, state policy makers have pursued different concepts of equity in designing and implementing their school funding systems. Some aim to weaken the link between per-pupil education resources and the per-pupil property wealth of school districts. Wealth neutrality would be achieved if per-pupil revenues supporting education—the sum of property tax levies and state aid—were completely uncorrelated with per-pupil property wealth. In an influential article, the economist Martin Feldstein (1975) demonstrated that as long as residents of high–property wealth school districts are willing to pay higher tax rates to support more education spending, no state-aid allocation can achieve wealth neutrality. The only way to achieve wealth neutrality would be through a completely state-funded school finance system.

Alternatively, state-aid systems could be designed to achieve equality of access. Under such a system, state aid would be allocated among school districts so that those with identical school property tax rates could spend the same amount of money per pupil, regardless of the size of their property tax base. Across a state, however, per-pupil education revenue would still depend on the property tax rate choices of local school districts.

Since the 1980s, most discussions of school funding equity have concentrated on the large variations in student academic performance. Many state supreme courts ruled that public education funding systems must guarantee all school districts sufficient funding to provide all their students what came to be known

as an adequate education. The courts mandated that states establish academic standards that met adequacy criteria.

Each school district has its own characteristics, including size, location, and the socioeconomic composition of its student body. Substantial evidence has shown that those characteristics dictate how much money school districts must spend to provide equal-quality education. Thus, school district per-pupil spending will differ for each school district. State-established academic standards for an adequate education, plus individual district characteristics, determine how much money a school district needs. School funding experts can calculate the cost of an adequate education based on these standards by estimating a cost function. Or they can use a non-statistical method such as the professional judgment approach, the successful districts approach, or the evidence-based approach (Downes and Stiefel 2015).

Why Is Defining Fairness in School Funding so Complicated?

When developing equitable school funding systems, state policy makers need to address several questions. First, fairness for whom—taxpayers or students? In a school funding system that relies heavily on local property taxes, taxpayers in property-poor jurisdictions will face much higher property tax rates than those in property-wealthy jurisdictions to raise the same amount of per-pupil revenue. Definitions of funding equity that prioritize taxpayers would deem such a system inequitable. Alternatively, definitions of equity prioritizing students would find inequities if large differences existed among jurisdictions in the resources flowing to students.

The second question is whether fairness in school funding relates to equity in educational inputs—revenues or spending—or to equity in educational outcomes.

Most early school finance litigation aimed to reduce educational inequities by concentrating on differences among school districts in per-pupil revenues or per-pupil spending. More recently, efforts have focused on reducing inequities in the quality of education provided to students. The goal of school funding reforms and recent litigation has been to ensure that all students receive a high-quality, or at least adequate, education.

The third question is whether the state should limit wealthy school districts' school spending. If school funding systems can guarantee that all school districts have sufficient revenues for all students to receive a good education, to what extent should states limit or prevent additional educational spending by some (presumably high-wealth) school districts?

In searching for a fair school funding system, one question is whether the focus should be fairness for taxpayers or students. *Source: monkeybusinessimages/iStock/Getty Images Plus*

Implicit in any discussion of adequate school funding is the assumption that additional fiscal resources will improve educational outcomes. Although most parents and educators, whether in low-income or high-income communities, take for granted that spending more money on their schools can make a positive difference, scholars have long debated whether money matters. The rich literature on the relationship between school spending and student outcomes generally concludes that it does (see "Money Matters" box on page 12).

The Property Tax– School Funding Dilemma

As a country, the United States' goal should be to maintain and strengthen a system of public education that provides all students high-quality schooling regardless of where they live. The two major sources of funding for public education—local property taxes and state aid—have weaknesses as well as strengths. Balancing these two revenue sources to finance K–12 education is not easy.

Funding through locally controlled property taxes promotes civic engagement and local involvement in K–12 education and can make spending more efficient. Meaningful local control requires at least some education funding to come from local sources. Many

characteristics of the property tax make it suitable as a local funding source: its tax base is immobile, which is important for a local tax, and it provides a more stable source of revenue over business cycles than do alternative taxes.

Despite its strengths, the property tax has its critics. One frequent complaint is that, using the same property tax rate, property-wealthy school districts can raise more tax revenue than other districts. Heavy reliance on the property tax, or for that matter any local tax, will allow wealthy school districts to spend more than poorer districts. Another complaint is that for some taxpayers, especially the elderly, property tax bills can be high relative to their incomes.

> Funding through locally controlled property taxes promotes civic engagement and local involvement in K–12 education and can make spending more efficient.

Well-designed state aid can compensate for the inequities created by differences among school districts in the value of per-pupil property tax bases. Increased state funding, however, is not guaranteed to be fair and sufficient for the poorest school districts to provide their students a high-quality education.

Money Matters

In an influential congressionally mandated study, the sociologist James Coleman and colleagues (1966) concluded that students' socioeconomic characteristics were much more important than school resources in explaining differences in student achievement. *Equality of Educational Opportunity,* known as the Coleman Report, spurred many statistical studies exploring the relationship between education resources and student outcomes. In several papers, including a widely read 2003 literature review, Eric Hanushek argued there is sparse evidence that spending more money leads to improved student outcomes, owing to statistical issues and inconsistent results. In a meta-analysis of most of the same studies, however, Hedges, Laine, and Greenwald (1994) reported a clear positive association between school spending and educational outcomes.

Statistical methods developed in this century and the availability of more detailed data on schooling have enabled researchers to generate plausible estimates of causal relationships between school resources, such as per-pupil spending, and outcomes, such as test scores, graduation rates, and in some cases post-education earnings. This new generation of empirical studies allows researchers to, for example, compare students before and after court-mandated school finance reforms or compare students in states with reforms with those in states without reforms. Jackson (2018, 13) reviewed recent literature and concluded that it "overwhelmingly supports a causal relationship between increased school spending and student outcomes."

In one such study, Hyman (2017) found that students exposed to a 10 percent increase in spending as a result of Michigan's 1994 school finance reform were 7 percent more likely to enroll in college and 11 percent more likely to earn a postsecondary degree.

And the greater the reliance on state aid, the larger the risk of funding cuts during recessions, when the major sources of state government tax revenue—sales and income taxes—are likely to decline.

Both the local property tax and state aid have problems; the dilemma is how to avoid each source's shortcomings while equitably and efficiently funding an adequate education for all students.

The COVID-19 pandemic brought new urgency to school funding, and the combination of pandemic-related school closures and the switch to remote learning led to substantial learning losses for many students. The pandemic took a particular toll on students from low-income families and students with physical and learning disabilities (Goldhaber et al. 2022). School districts received substantial federal aid for pandemic-related expenditures, and funding to ameliorate learning losses will likely need to continue after the extra federal funding ends in 2024. School funding systems will be pressured to replace federal funds with additional funding from the property tax and state aid and to allocate these funds to remedy disparities in student performance that have likely increased during the pandemic.

The COVID-19 pandemic brought new urgency to school funding, and the combination of pandemic-related school closures and the switch to remote learning led to substantial learning losses for many students.

CHAPTER 2

Funding K–12 Education:
The Local Property Tax and Its Alternatives

The property tax endures as the dominant source of local funding for schools, though reliance on it can vary among school districts and among states. By its nature, the property tax is well suited for local governments: it is efficient, stable, and usually preserves local control. Property wealth per pupil can vary by district, however, and disparities arise among school districts. To address some of these challenges, all 50 states offer direct relief to households, and most states have enacted property tax limits. These policies have spurred some municipal and county governments—though rarely school districts— to shift to alternative sources of local funding.

New Hampshire derives 61 percent of its K–12 school revenue from local property taxes—the highest reliance in the nation. *Source: DenisTangneyJr/iStock/Getty Images Plus*

Variation in Property Tax Reliance

Reliance on the local property tax to fund schools varies by state. In New England, local property taxes account for about half or more of total revenue for public schools except in Vermont, which derives most of its revenue from a state-levied property tax. In contrast, Hawaii's centralized school finance system relies entirely on state revenue. In 14 other states, local property tax revenues provide less than a quarter of total funding for schools, as shown in figure 2.1.

Local property tax reliance varies among not only states but also school districts within a state. The size of each district's property tax base and the size of its public school student population affect how easily districts can fund education with the local property tax. Voter preferences can also affect reliance on local property taxes.

How the Property Tax Works

The property tax base is the value of taxable real and personal property. Real property includes land and permanent improvements like houses and office buildings, and it makes up the largest share of the property tax base. State and local governments levy property taxes on residential and nonresidential property in all 50 states.

Because the true market value of property is known only if it has recently been sold, state, county, or local governments must estimate the market value of each parcel in their jurisdiction to start determining the property tax. Governments make adjustments to arrive at a property's assessed value, then divide the amount of revenue to be raised by the total assessed value of property in the jurisdiction to calculate the tax rate. Each taxpayer's gross tax liability is calculated

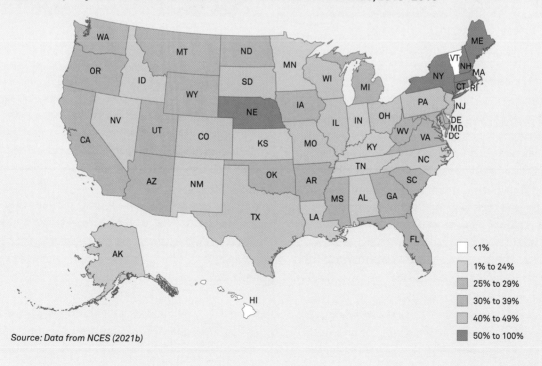

Figure 2.1

Local Property Tax Revenue as a Share of Public Education Revenue, 2018–2019

Legend:
- <1%
- 1% to 24%
- 25% to 29%
- 30% to 39%
- 40% to 49%
- 50% to 100%

Source: Data from NCES (2021b)

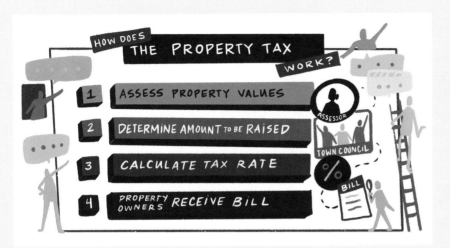

LEARN MORE

For a fuller explanation of how the property tax works, watch the Lincoln Institute's explainer video, "Property Tax 101: The Mechanics" and read Ronald C. Fisher's "Property Taxes: What Everybody Needs to Know" (2021).

by multiplying the assessed value of the taxpayer's property by the applicable rate. Actual tax liabilities are determined by adjusting the gross liabilities for applicable exemptions and credits.

Who Pays the Property Tax

Taxing jurisdictions levy property taxes on residential, commercial, and industrial property. Property owned by the government and by charitable nonprofits is generally exempt from taxation.

Determining who actually pays the property tax (for example, tenants or their landlords) is difficult and has led to conflicting conclusions about the incidence of the property tax. When a tax is progressive, higher-income taxpayers pay a larger share of their income than lower-income taxpayers pay. When a tax is proportional, taxpayers of different income levels pay about the same share of their incomes. When a tax is regressive, lower-income taxpayers pay a higher share of their income than higher-income taxpayers do. The traditional, once prevailing, view of the property tax asserts it is a tax on housing and consumption; from this perspective, the property tax is somewhat regressive, because lower-income

households spend a greater share of their income on housing. Today, most economists view the property tax as a tax on capital. Because higher-income taxpayers own larger shares of capital, the property tax is more progressive under this view. An analysis of several studies on tax incidence holding different views found that, in either case, the property tax is generally proportional or progressive, but it may be regressive for the lowest-income groups (Fisher 2016).

Property Tax Challenges

Though ideal for funding education for the reasons described in chapter 1, the property tax is imperfect. The assessed value of property within a school district or community—that is, the property tax base—varies from district to district. Property wealth determines how much a school district can raise at a given property tax rate. We can compare school districts' property wealth by dividing the assessed value of property in each district by the number of students enrolled in its schools.

Consider two hypothetical school districts, each with a student population of 100. The total assessed value of all property in District A is $30 million, and the total value of all property in District B is $60 million. In this example, District A has $300,000 of property value per pupil, and District B has $600,000 of property value per pupil.

If each district wants to raise $500,000 ($5,000 per pupil) through local property taxation, District A must levy a property tax rate of $16.67 per $1,000 of assessed value, but District B will require a rate of only $8.33 per $1,000. Alternatively, if both school districts choose to tax property at a rate of $16.67 per $1,000 of assessed value, District B will raise $10,000 per pupil in property tax revenue. In this scenario, an owner of a home valued at $300,000 will pay $5,000 in either district, but assuming no state aid, District B would be able to spend twice as much per pupil as District A, as shown in table 2.1.

Table 2.1

Hypothetical School District Funding Disparity

	District A	District B
Student Population	100	100
Local Property Value	$30,000,000	$60,000,000
Property Wealth (local property value per pupil)	$300,000 per Pupil	$600,000 per Pupil
Tax Rate Required to Raise $500,000	$16.67 per $1,000 Assessed Value	$8.33 per $1,000 Assessed Value
Revenue Raised at $16.67 per $1,000 Assessed Value	$500,000	$1,000,000
Revenue Raised per Pupil at a Tax Rate of $16.67 per $1,000 Assessed Value	$5,000	$10,000
Per-Pupil State Aid Required to Equalize per-Pupil Spending	$5,000	$0

As described in chapter 3, states can target aid to help equalize these interdistrict disparities. In this hypothetical example, a state-aid formula that distributes an additional $5,000 per student to District A will equalize per-pupil spending in the two districts.

Unlike the sales tax, which residents pay in small increments, or the income tax, which is withheld from each paycheck for most workers, the property tax generally requires payment in one or two lump sums.

Because property taxes are based on property values rather than income, low-income taxpayers or those who suffer a sudden loss of income often face a high tax burden relative to their income. For example, homeowners who lose their jobs will pay less in income taxes, but their property tax bill will not decline. Elderly homeowners whose home values have appreciated over a long period but whose incomes have declined could pay a high share of their income in property taxes.

In a jurisdiction with a well-administered property tax system, taxpayers living in similar houses should receive similar tax bills. However, in some jurisdictions, especially those that reassess property values infrequently, the link between the tax bill and a property's market value can be broken. Taxpayers with similar houses similarly situated within a jurisdiction can face very different property tax bills. In some cases, these horizontal inequities—unequal treatment of equals—result from public policies such as state-imposed assessment limits.

Unlike the sales tax, which residents pay in small increments, or the income tax, which is withheld from each paycheck for most workers, the property tax generally requires payment in one or two lump

Michigan's Homestead Property Tax Credit is a circuit breaker program that provides property tax relief to households with incomes less than $60,000 and bases the benefit on the taxpayer's property tax burden relative to income. *Source: Peeter Viisimaa/ iStock/Getty Images Plus*

sums. For most mortgaged residential properties, the bank makes payments to the local government on behalf of the mortgagee from an escrow account into which these homeowners make monthly payments. But for taxpayers without escrow accounts, particularly if they are low- and moderate-income homeowners, large lump-sum payments may require advance planning and can create economic hardships (Langley 2018).

Policies to Address Challenges

States have addressed some of the shortcomings of the property tax by providing direct relief to households meeting set criteria. These include homestead exemptions and credits, circuit breakers, deferrals, and monthly installments. Langley and Youngman (2021) investigate residential property tax relief in detail.

HOMESTEAD EXEMPTIONS AND CREDITS

Homestead exemptions and credits are the most widespread form of direct residential property tax relief. A homestead exemption reduces the assessed value of primary homes by a fixed dollar amount or percentage of value. In most states, owner-occupied primary residences benefit from homestead exemptions. In some states, homestead exemptions are limited to seniors, veterans, disabled taxpayers, or other select groups.

PROPERTY TAX CIRCUIT BREAKERS

A circuit breaker program is tax relief that reduces tax liability for taxpayers with a high property tax

Taxpayers in Milwaukee, Wisconsin, can pay their property taxes in monthly installments. *Source: peeterv/iStock/ Getty Images*

burden relative to income. The direct relief increases as household income declines. For example, a claimant may receive a credit equal to the amount by which the property tax bill exceeds 10 percent of income. Unlike homestead exemptions that provide relief to entire groups of households (such as elderly or veterans) or property tax limitations that restrict property taxes for all taxpayers regardless of ability to pay, circuit breakers target aid to overburdened taxpayers (Bowman et al. 2009). Thirty-one states and the District of Columbia had at least one property tax circuit breaker program in 2020 (Lincoln Institute of Land Policy 2022).

Circuit breaker programs increase the progressivity of the property tax by reducing tax burdens on lower-income households without diminishing property tax revenue from households with average or low tax burdens relative to income. However, the efficiency and effectiveness of property tax circuit breaker programs depends on their design.

DEFERRALS

Deferral programs allow eligible taxpayers (usually senior citizens) to put off property tax payments until they die or sell their property. Upon sale or transfer, the deferred property taxes become payable with interest. Deferrals are designed to address a mismatch between high property taxes and low annual income. Tax deferral programs, which are similar to reverse-equity mortgages, are not widely used.

MONTHLY INSTALLMENTS

Highly visible, large annual or semiannual payments may contribute to the unpopularity of the property tax. Some states and jurisdictions have adopted policies to allow property owners without escrow accounts to pay property taxes in monthly installments (Langley 2018).

Property Tax Limits

State governments in 46 states and the District of Columbia constrain increases in local property taxes through constitutional or statutory limits on growth in property tax rates, levies, assessments, or some mixture of these (Paquin 2015a). Most state-imposed property tax limits contain provisions by which the governing body can override the limit, typically by a simple-majority or supermajority vote. Overrides relieve local governments from the limits when local residents support higher spending.

Property tax limits take several forms:

- **Rate limits** cap property tax rates and may apply to the tax rate of specific jurisdictions, such as a school district, or to the overall rate of overlying jurisdictions, such as the combined tax rate of the county, municipality, and school district. Texas, for example, limits most school district maintenance and operations property tax rates to $1.17 per $100 of assessed value. Rate limits do not prevent property taxes from rising as values rise unless combined with an assessment limit. Thirty-four states and the District of Columbia imposed rate limits in 2020, though school districts were excluded from some limits (Lincoln Institute of Land Policy and GWIPP).

- **Assessment limits** cap annual increases in property assessments by freezing assessed values or limiting their growth. In some states, reassessment to market value occurs only when a property is sold, a policy known as acquisition value assessment. California limits annual increases in assessed value to 2 percent or the rate of inflation, whichever is less, regardless of changes in market value. Because California also limits property tax rates to 1 percent, property tax increases are highly constrained. Assessment limits lead to wide disparities in tax bills for owners of similar properties, which tends to discourage mobility. In 2020, 17 states and the District of Columbia imposed limits on property tax assessments (Lincoln Institute and GWIPP 2022).

- **Levy limits** cap a jurisdiction's growth in property tax revenues. Because levy limits restrict the total property tax revenue jurisdictions can raise, they are more restrictive as a standalone limit than are limits for rates or assessments. However, levy limits do not distort the relationship between market value and tax liability. New York's Property Tax Cap law, implemented in 2011, limits growth in school district and local government property tax levies (excluding spending for pensions and school district capital, and court orders) to 2 percent per year or the rate of inflation, whichever is less. School districts and local governments can override the limit with approval by 60 percent of voters, or 60 percent of the governing body for local governments. A 2021 study found that reduced revenue caused by the cap resulted in drops in student academic performance (Sorensen, Kim, and Hwang 2021). Thirty-six states and the District of Columbia imposed levy limits in 2020, though not all levy limits apply to school districts (Lincoln Institute and GWIPP 2022).

Other types of tax and expenditure limits do not exclusively and directly constrain property taxes. Revenue limits and expenditure limits that restrict a jurisdiction's total revenues or annual spending can restrict the allowable property taxation.

A limit is binding if it restricts property taxes, but a standalone limit on property tax rates is not considered binding, because local governments can circumvent it by altering assessment practices.

The stringency of a tax limit depends on its design. A limit is binding if it restricts property taxes, but a standalone limit on property tax rates is not considered binding, because local governments can circumvent it by altering assessment practices (Mullins and Cox 1995; Paquin 2015b). To learn more about property tax limits, see "State-Imposed Property Tax Limitations: Trends and Outlook" (Paquin 2015b) and "Chronicle of the 161-Year History of State-Imposed Property Tax Limitations" (Paquin 2015a).

Alternatives to the Local Property Tax

In most states, the property tax is the only broad-based tax that independent school districts can levy, and it supplies 80 percent of local revenues for K–12 education (NCES 2021b).

As Langley and Youngman (2021) explain, disparities among taxing jurisdictions are not unique to the property tax but rather a challenge of local taxation generally. Local sales and income taxes are subject to the same interjurisdictional equity issues due to variation in the size of tax bases. As described in chapter 1, local income and sales taxes are less stable than the property tax and easier to avoid. However, when property tax limits and other policies hamper growth in property tax revenue, alternative revenue sources can help fill the gap.

Seventeen states plus the District of Columbia rely on local sources other than the property tax for more than 10 percent of total revenue for schools; those sources include local sales and income taxes, fees, charges, charitable giving, and revenue from private sources (NCES 2021b). In 12 states and the District of Columbia, local sales taxes or income taxes make up 5 percent or more of total local revenue for schools, as figure 2.2 shows. Local sales and income tax revenues generally come from local option taxes and are not necessarily levied by all school districts within a state.

Figure 2.2

States with Local Sales or Income Taxes Used for Education

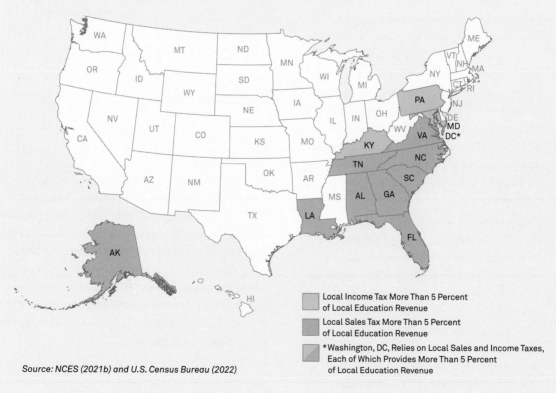

Local Income Tax More Than 5 Percent of Local Education Revenue

Local Sales Tax More Than 5 Percent of Local Education Revenue

*Washington, DC, Relies on Local Sales and Income Taxes, Each of Which Provides More Than 5 Percent of Local Education Revenue

Source: NCES (2021b) and U.S. Census Bureau (2022)

Louisiana is the only state in which local sales taxes provide more funding for schools than the property tax. *Source: Sean Pavone/iStock Editorial/Getty Images Plus*

LOCAL SALES TAXES

School districts in nine states and the District of Columbia rely on local sales taxes for 5 percent or more of local K–12 education revenue. In some of these states, like Alaska and North Carolina, all school districts depend on parent local governments that levy local sales taxes. Louisiana is one of the few states in which independent school districts can tax sales and is also the state that raises the largest share of local education funding through local sales taxes. In Louisiana's fiscal year 2019, local sales taxes contributed 21 percent of total funding for independent school districts; property tax revenue contributed about 19 percent (U.S. Census Bureau 2020).

LOCAL INCOME TAXES

Local income taxes make up 5 percent or more of K–12 revenue in three states plus the District of Columbia. Independent school districts in Kentucky and Maryland rely on local income taxes, and Maryland's dependent school districts rely on local income taxes collected by their parent governments. Municipalities authorized to tax income typically levy the tax on the wages and salaries of residents of the jurisdiction and in some cases, of nonresidents who work in the jurisdiction (Sjoquist and Stephenson 2010).

FEES AND CHARGES

Most school districts raise some revenue from user fees and charges. Fees are generally limited to noneducational activities of school districts, like school lunches, student activities, and transportation. In FY 2019–2020, fees and charges made up only 4 percent of independent school districts' locally raised revenues (U.S. Census Bureau 2022). In a study of nontax revenues, Downes and Killeen (2014) found that even during the Great Recession, when school property tax revenues declined, school district revenues from fees and charges remained largely unchanged.

CHARITABLE CONTRIBUTIONS

Charitable contributions are another nontax alternative revenue source for public schools. The most common school-supporting nonprofits are school-level parent-teacher organizations, alumni associations, booster clubs, school foundations, and local endowments. Charitable donations to public schools account for a very small share of revenue. In 2019, all private local funding sources for public schools (charitable donations plus tuition and fees paid by students living outside the district) accounted for just 1.6 percent of total school revenues nationwide; gift revenues tend to be unevenly distributed (NCES 2021a; Nelson and Gazley 2014).

STATE-LEVIED PROPERTY TAXES

Some states use a state-levied property tax to supplement local funding and reduce disparities among school districts. In levying a uniform property tax across the state, states benefit from the stability and transparency of the property tax base. By targeting this revenue to the neediest school districts, states can use the property tax to reduce interdistrict disparities, increasing the equity of the school funding system. However, with a statewide levy, local school districts have no say in setting the tax rate.

Seven states (Alabama, Kansas, Michigan, Montana, Minnesota, Vermont, and Washington) levy their own property tax and dedicate all or some of the revenue to K–12 education (Haveman 2020).

Pandemic Effect on Commercial Property Values and Property Taxes

Initial research suggests the COVID-19 pandemic's impact on real estate and, in turn, property taxes, may outlast the public health crisis. The lockdowns and stay-at-home orders in March 2020 triggered a mass shift toward remote work for many U.S. workers, especially those in large cities, a trend that researchers predict will persist.

Ramani and Bloom (2021) find the pandemic has pushed workers and businesses out of city centers to suburbs, a phenomenon the researchers call the "donut effect," with real estate prices rising in the suburbs and falling in city centers as more people work from home. They observe patterns consistent with hybrid work-from-home arrangements (two days per week), rather than full-time work from home. Ramani and Bloom warn that major cities could see "persistent" reductions in tax collections because of this shift.

Chernick, Copeland, and Merriman (2021) also predict a long-term fiscal risk to cities from the pandemic

recession. Many of the commercial sectors in the eight large cities they study are composed of industries in which most workers can do their jobs from home. On average, 37 percent of prepandemic property tax revenues in those cities came from commercial properties. The authors find that the larger the share of industries that are highly adaptable to remote work, the greater the impact on commercial property demand and values. They estimate a 12 to 25 percent drop in commercial property values (including rental housing) and a commensurate decline in property tax revenues. They assume property tax rates do not change and employees continue to work from home at the current rate in a two- or three-day hybrid work-from-home arrangement. Fewer in-person workers further reduces the demand for commercial property in cities, depressing commercial property values and shrinking the commercial property tax base.

Conversely, residential home values across the country appreciated rapidly during the pandemic, creating an estimated $6 trillion in wealth for U.S. homeowners in a two-year span (Board of Governors of the U.S. Federal Reserve System 2022). Mark Zandi, chief economist for Moody's, predicted in 2022 that the historic growth in home equity would endure, pointing to a housing shortage and demand fueled in part by low mortgage rates and footloose remote workers (Badger and Bui 2022).

Manhattan office building values declined 25 percent from 2021 to 2022, and researchers estimate that two-thirds of the decline was due to more employees working from home—a trend that is likely to persist post COVID-19 pandemic. *Source: Richard Levine/ Alamy Stock Photo*

CHAPTER 3
State Education Aid

State aid and revenue from property taxes are the two main funding sources for U.S. public education. State aid is crucial in reducing funding inequities due to spatially uneven property tax bases. If state-aid systems are well designed, they are powerful in reducing academic achievement gaps between poor and nonpoor students. Although the goals of most state-aid programs are similar, their design and implementation vary widely among states. Not surprisingly, large funding inequities between and within states persist.

State funding formulas often use weights to adjust for the higher cost of educating students with disabilities, limited English proficiency, or low income. *Source: FatCamera/Getty Images/E+*

The roles state governments play in financing elementary and secondary education differ widely. Thirteen state governments in school year 2018–2019 contributed less than 40 percent of total revenue, as seen in figure 3.1, and in 11 states that share was more than 60 percent. A strong inverse relationship exists between the funding role of state governments and states' reliance on property taxation: in states that provided more than 60 percent of education funding, except for Delaware, the property tax accounted for less than 25 percent of total school revenues.

Goals of State Aid

State constitutions in all but two states require state government to support education. State aid not only funds education but also partially substitutes for local property taxes in most states, thereby providing property tax relief to residents and businesses.

Without state aid, spatial differences in per-pupil property tax bases and in education costs would cause large differences in the resources for public education's funding and quality. Central to every state's policies is the goal of reducing these differences. States place differing importance on equity and adequacy goals. In the last several decades, most states have sought to reduce differences in student academic outcomes by ensuring that each school district has sufficient resources to provide its students an adequate education. In many states, school funding policy promotes equality of access, which loosens the tie between property tax rates and the total amount of per-pupil resources. Some states place limits on property tax rates or per-pupil spending by property-wealthy school districts.

Figure 3.1

State Share of Public Education Revenue, 2018–2019

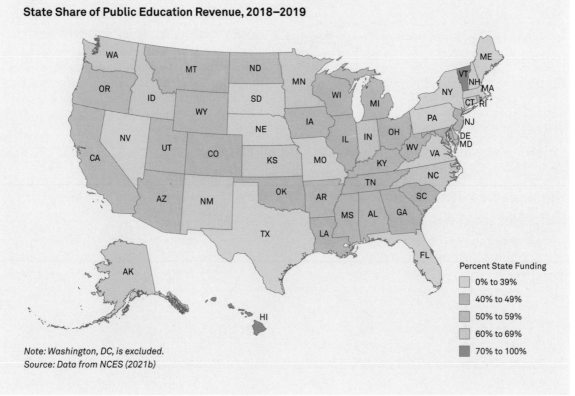

Percent State Funding

- 0% to 39%
- 40% to 49%
- 50% to 59%
- 60% to 69%
- 70% to 100%

Note: Washington, DC, is excluded.
Source: Data from NCES (2021b)

Many states, including Arizona, provide sparsity aid to rural school districts to compensate low-enrollment districts for higher per-pupil operating costs. *Source: Maxiphoto/iStock/Getty Images Plus*

State governments in five states spent less than $5,000 per pupil in FY 2020, while eight states and the District of Columbia spent more than $10,000 per pupil (U.S. Census Bureau 2022). Most school funding systems are quite complex, and aid is allocated using different formulas, each designed to achieve a specific goal. The next section explains the design of the two types of formulas used most frequently.

State Aid to Achieve School Funding Equity Goals

FOUNDATION FORMULAS

A foundation formula calculates how much state aid a school district needs to reach a state's mandated per-pupil spending, or foundation level. Many states (34 in 2021) use cost-adjusted foundation formulas to allocate state education aid, and several others combine a foundation formula with other formulas (Fischer, Duncombe, and Syverson 2021). Foundation aid is the difference between a state-determined foundation level of per-pupil spending and the amount of money per pupil a school district receives if it uses a state-mandated property tax rate. School districts that raise more property tax revenue than the foundation level receive no foundation aid. In most states, school districts are allowed to increase spending above the foundation level by choosing property tax rates higher than the state-mandated rate. To reduce inequalities among school districts, some states set limits on how much districts can spend above the foundation level.

A foundation level and a required tax rate are state government policy decisions. In some states, these decisions appear to be driven primarily by budgetary and other political concerns. In other states, foundation levels are explicitly based on an estimate of the average per-pupil cost of providing an adequate education. For example, studies largely determined the foundation levels for Arkansas and North Dakota (Picus, Goertz, and Odden 2015). Some states use student-teacher ratios or other algorithms to determine the number of teachers and other teaching resources each school district requires. A district's foundation level is then determined by the average cost of the required resources.

How a Foundation Formula Works

Figure 3.2 illustrates a foundation formula in a state where school district per-pupil property values range from $200,000 to $1.2 million. Assume that the state legislature defines the foundation level of school spending at $10,000 per pupil (F*) and the required property tax rate at 1 percent. Per-pupil foundation aid (the area in red) is the difference between the foundation level and the property tax revenue (the area in blue). The poorest district in the state (in terms of property wealth) raises $2,000 in per-pupil property tax revenue. Foundation aid of $8,000 per pupil fills the gap to reach the $10,000 foundation level. A school district with a per-pupil property tax base of $800,000 can raise $8,000 in property taxes per pupil and is entitled to a $2,000-per-pupil foundation grant.

School districts with per-pupil property wealth of $1 million or more can raise more than $10,000 per pupil at the mandated rate and hence receive no foundation aid. All school districts are allowed to choose property tax rates higher than the mandated rate, thus spending above the foundation level (the area in green). As shown in figure 3.2, only school districts with tax bases larger than $500,000 per pupil choose to do so.

Figure 3.2

Hypothetical Foundation Aid Formula

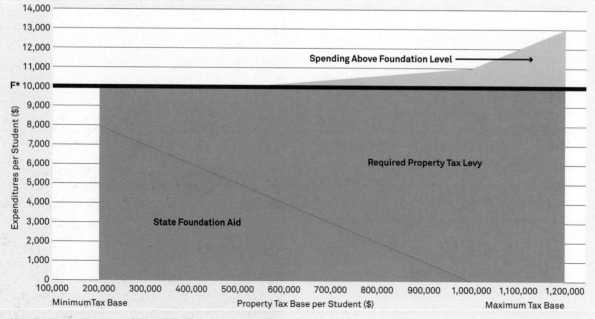

Note: Foundation level (F) is $10,000; required tax rate is 1 percent.*

Regardless of how a state determines it, a foundation level must be regularly updated to reflect increases in the cost of education. Failure to do so as costs rise not only increases funding inequities but also, as property values rise, reduces total foundation aid and the state government's share of total education funding.

In 2001, Congress enacted No Child Left Behind, which mandated annual testing of all students in grades three through eight and required that schools make annual progress in meeting student performance standards for all students and for separate groups of students classified by race, ethnicity, poverty, disability, and limited English proficiency (U.S. Department of Education 2002). How to assess student achievement and how to define standards for adequate academic performance were left up to each state. Academic adequacy standards thus differ among states.

GUARANTEED TAX BASE FORMULAS

States pursuing equality of access define a guaranteed per-pupil tax base so that the sum of a district's state and local revenues depends only on its chosen property tax rate and not on the size of its tax base. A guaranteed tax base (GTB) formula determines a district's state-aid allocation, which is the difference between (1) the revenue that would be raised at a district's chosen property tax rate if its tax base equaled the GTB and (2) the revenue raised from its actual tax base. Because the size of the GTB grant is proportional to a school district's chosen property tax rate, it is a matching grant, and the matching rate is greater for school districts with lower per-pupil property tax bases.

School districts with a per-pupil property tax base larger than the GTB have a negative matching rate. To achieve full equality of access with a GTB formula, those districts would return a portion of their property tax revenue to the state. Currently, no state requires these negative aid payments.

COMBINATION FORMULAS

Several states combine a foundation formula with a GTB formula. A GTB formula ensures that the state's share of funding above the foundation level is larger for school districts with lower per-student property wealth. As described in chapter 4, Texas and Wisconsin supplement foundation aid with GTB aid, but both states disincentivize additional spending by property-wealthy districts.

Adjusting State Aid for Within-State Variations in the Costs of Education

A foundation level sets the average per-pupil spending a state needs to achieve educational adequacy. However, the minimum amount of money varies among school districts, reflecting differences in student backgrounds and in the size and location of school districts. To some extent, these cost factors are reflected in all state-aid systems.

To account for these differences, state aid is adjusted according to the proportion of high-cost students in a district, usually by replacing actual student counts with weighted student counts. The weights reflect the higher costs associated with educating particular groups of students. Weights are most commonly used for students with mental or physical disabilities who participate in special education programs, students with limited English proficiency, and students from low-income families.

For students with disabilities, weights usually vary by type of disability, with weights for severe disabilities generally far exceeding 2.0. Research based on the statistical estimation of education cost functions or on the collective judgment of panels of education professionals find poverty weights usually greater than 0.5 and frequently larger than 1.0 (Duncombe, Nhuyen-Hoang, and Yinger 2015; Duncombe and Yinger

Consider a school district with 1,000 students, half of them from low-income families. If the state-aid system assigns an extra weight of 0.35 to all students from poor families, the weighted number of students would be 1,175 [1,000 + (500 × 0.35)]. Now assume that the state-aid formula allocates $5,000 per pupil. Without pupil weighting, the school district would receive $5 million in state aid ($5,000 × 1,000). With pupil weighting, the school district's state aid would be $5,875,000 ($5,000 × 1,175).

2005). In practice, however, poverty weights used in state-aid formulas tend to be considerably lower. In 2019, the modal weight was 0.25 (Dachelet 2019), but weights vary substantially across the United States. Research has suggested that the cost of educating students from low-income families increases with the concentration of poverty in a community (Reschovsky and Imazeki 1998). Eight states use higher poverty weights when the percentage of economically disadvantaged students rises above a specified threshold (EdBuild 2022).

Some states provide categorical grants for high-cost students. These grants are for specific purposes, such as special education or bilingual education programs. The size of each district's categorical grant is typically related to the number of students eligible for the educational programs financed by the categorical grant. Because some school districts might inflate that number, some states use a census-based system that allocates categorical aid in proportion to overall student enrollment.

Because small school districts are unable to exploit economies of scale, the per-pupil cost of education is higher in districts with fewer students (Duncombe and Yinger 2007; Imazeki and Reschovsky 2004). In rural areas, where a single school district can cover hundreds of square miles, school district consolidation is simply not feasible. To compensate these low-enrollment districts for unavoidable higher costs, many states provide additional aid, sometimes referred to as sparsity aid.

Some states adjust aid to reflect differences among school districts in the salary and benefits needed to attract high-quality educators. These differences arise because the cost of living can vary substantially within states. Several states, including Texas, use a comparable wage index to adjust aid for geographic variations in employment-related costs. The index estimates the wages a typical college graduate not employed in K–12 education would earn in different local labor markets (Taylor and Fowler 2006).

Performance of State Aid

The National Assessment of Educational Progress (NAEP), administered by the U.S. Department of Education, is the nation's only representative and ongoing test of student academic performance. The percentage of fourth- and eighth-grade public school students scoring at or above proficient levels on the 2019 NAEP reading and mathematics exams varied tremendously by state. Not only was the range in scores wide, but student performance was at least 10 percent higher or lower than the national average in many states—between 19 and 36 states, depending on grade and subject. Although state rankings differ by test and grade level, states that score well (or poorly) on one test tend to perform well (or poorly) on other tests.

Evaluating school funding systems in terms of equity and adequacy goals is a complex undertaking. Isolating the impacts of state aid from the impacts of other elements is particularly challenging. Nevertheless, in recent years, scholars and organizations have assessed the performance of states' school funding systems.

In our view, the studies most closely linked to the adequacy and equity goals we discuss here are published by the Albert Shanker Institute and the Rutgers University Graduate School of Education (see, e.g., Baker et al. 2021). Their annual reports calculate three school funding performance indicators: adequacy, fiscal effort, and progressivity. Chapter 5 includes definitions of these measures and uses them to assess school funding systems in five states.

Districts across the country, including the Anaheim Elementary School District in California, incurred significant expense in retrofitting classrooms to safely allow students to return to school during the pandemic. *Source: Photo by Paul Bersebach/Orange County Register via Getty Images*

State Aid and the Macroeconomy

Aid to elementary and secondary schools is the largest single item in most states' general fund budgets. For this reason, and because state governments must balance their budgets, state aid is particularly sensitive to changes in state government tax revenues. From 2007 to 2010, the years straddling the Great Recession, state government tax revenue in the United States declined by 11.4 percent after adjusting for inflation. According to the Center on Budget and Policy Priorities, formula-based state aid per pupil was lower in school year 2011–2012, after adjusting for inflation, than it had been in 2007–2008 in 30 of the 46 states

for which they had data (Oliff and Leachman 2011). In more than half these 30 states, cuts were greater than 10 percent.

Several researchers have investigated the impact of the Great Recession on equity in school funding. Evans, Schwab, and Wagner (2019) found that after several decades of decline in both within- and between-state inequality in per-pupil spending, it began to increase starting in 2000. Between 2000 and 2013, between-state per-pupil spending inequality rose by 86 percent and within-state inequality by 21 percent. The researchers conclude that the sharp drop in state education aid that occurred in most states during and after the Great Recession likely contributed to this rising inequality in per-student spending. Shores and Steinberg (2019) suggest that cuts in state aid may have exacerbated spending inequalities because, whereas high-income or high-property-wealth school districts can offset cuts in state aid by increasing locally raised revenues, low-property-wealth districts are less able to offset reductions.

State policy makers could minimize the likelihood of large spending cuts during recessions by accumulating rainy-day funds during periods of economic growth.

State policy makers could minimize the likelihood of large spending cuts during recessions by building up rainy-day funds during periods of economic growth. At the end of states' FY 2021, the median rainy-day balance was 9.4 percent of general fund expenditures (NASBO 2021). State balances, however, varied tremendously from the median. In 10 states, balances were 5 percent or less of spending, and in 15 states they exceeded 15 percent.

Federal Aid

The federal government has long played a role in funding public elementary and secondary education, although a relatively small one compared with that of governments in most other countries. Except for three years right after the Great Recession, when public education benefited from federal stimulus spending, federal prepandemic education revenues never exceeded 10 percent. In FY 2019, the federal share was 7.8 percent.

Federal aid to elementary and secondary education is allocated through a set of categorical grants. The largest grant program is Title I of the Every Student Succeeds Act of 2015. School districts receive additional resources for children from economically disadvantaged families. The second-largest program helps fund special education programs for students with disabilities as mandated by the federal Individuals with Disabilities Education Act (passed in 1975, reauthorized in 1990).

The COVID-19 Pandemic

At the beginning of the pandemic, most schools closed and quickly transitioned to remote learning. Teachers had to adapt to a new mode of instruction and students to a new method of learning. The academic results were decidedly mixed: many students, especially those from low-income families, struggled to obtain internet access on appropriate electronic devices and to find quiet and uninterrupted locations for "attending" school.

Even after schools reopened, education was frequently interrupted by localized COVID-19 outbreaks that required quarantines and hybrid instruction. Early evidence has documented substantial learning losses by many students and suggests that the pandemic exacerbated existing disparities in student academic achievement. Data also suggest the negative impacts of the pandemic have been particularly severe for students of color, English-language learners, and special education students.

The pandemic also imposed large fiscal challenges on the nation's school districts. Schools had to quickly enable remote learning and then retrofit classrooms to allow a safe reopening. Many schools took on the additional tasks of providing many of their students internet access and delivering hot meals. Schools further face the complicated job of addressing the learning losses suffered by many students.

Fortunately, the federal government responded to the financial needs of schools with an unprecedented $190 billion earmarked for public education; however, that COVID-19 relief aid must be spent by late 2024, and many educators fear that making up for the learning loss due to the pandemic will remain a long-term problem requiring the investment of significant resources well beyond 2024. Whether additional state aid or property tax revenues will be forthcoming is an open question.

Declining Enrollment due to the Pandemic

When the COVID-19 pandemic thrust schools into remote and hybrid learning, public schools lost enrollment. For the 2020–2021 school year, enrollment was down 3 percent nationwide, compared with 2019–2020 levels. Declines were uneven among states and student groups, with the largest drops among pre–K and kindergarten students and among low-income and minority students (NCES 2021c). When schools switched to remote learning, some children were unable to access content, others failed to engage, and many moved to alternatives such as homeschooling and private schools (Korman, O'Keefe, and Repka 2020).

State aid for public schools is based on the number of students attending or enrolled, so a slump in attendance or enrollment can reduce revenue to schools. In response to pandemic-related enrollment declines, many states adopted short-term policies to hold school districts harmless if student numbers declined. Some states provided extra funding for school districts with declining enrollment (Delaware Department of Education 2020; Minnesota Rural Education Association 2021). Many states used prepandemic enrollment to calculate state aid (Fensterwald 2021). To bolster in-person learning, Texas even sent funding to districts that lost attendance if they maintained or increased in-person enrollment (Texas Office of the Governor 2021).

Pandemic-induced school closures and shifts to hybrid learning led to declines in enrollment, especially among the youngest students, students with low incomes, and minority students. Juanita Elementary School in Kirkland, Washington, displayed a message of support as its students shifted to remote learning. *Source: ColleenMichaels/Dreamstime.com*

CHAPTER 4

State Case Studies

A taxpayer revolt in California fueled the 1978 passage of Proposition 13, which limited growth in tax rates and assessments. *Source: Tony Korody/Getty Images*

The five case studies in this chapter illustrate the nuances of state education finance and property tax policies and offer important lessons for policy makers. These narratives on school funding in California, Massachusetts, South Carolina, Texas, and Wisconsin highlight each state's level of reliance on property tax and state aid, education finance history and related litigation, major school finance reforms, and current challenges.

As shown in table 4.1 (page 34), Massachusetts public schools rely heavily on the local property tax; it accounts for 52 percent of revenue, and 39 percent comes from the state. In California public schools, in contrast, just 27 percent of revenue comes from local property taxes. Among the five states, K–12 public school spending varies dramatically, from $17,748 in Massachusetts (seventh highest in the United States) to $9,827 in Texas (less than that of 43 states). Nationally, spending per pupil ranged from $7,950 in Utah to $24,882 in New York (NCES 2021a).

In all states, the share of students scoring at or above proficiency varies by race.

The states studied in this chapter confront very different demographic challenges: varying population growth rates, racial diversity, and child poverty. In Massachusetts and Wisconsin, more than half of public school students are white; in South Carolina about half of students are white, and in California and Texas, fewer than 30 percent of public school students are white. The share of school-age children living in poverty ranges from 18.7 percent in South Carolina to 11 percent in Massachusetts.

Massachusetts leads the nation in student achievement as measured by NAEP scores. In all states, the share of students scoring at or above proficiency varies by race. The race gaps in the bottom panel of table 4.1 (page 34) show the differences between the average score of white students and that of non-white students. For the United States as a whole, Black fourth-grade students score 25 points lower than white students on math, and Hispanic students score 18 points lower than their white peers. The Black-white math achievement gap is larger than the national average in California, South Carolina, and Wisconsin.

California: Property Tax Limits and Shift to State Funding

The history of school finance in California illustrates the tension between equity goals and tax reduction goals, and the unintended consequences of abandoning local funding of schools and of imposing assessment limits. In its pursuit of educational equity, California shifted funding away from local governments at the cost of local control. In taxpayers' quest to control property tax increases, they traded horizontal equity and fairness for predictability.

California educates more students than any other state in the country, in 1,000-plus independent school districts and 57 county-dependent school districts (U.S. Census Bureau 2019). Its student population is diverse, with white students accounting for just 22 percent of California public school students and Hispanic students exceeding 55 percent. Per-pupil spending is about average, at $14,035 per student in the 2018–2019 school year.

HIGHLY CENTRALIZED SCHOOL FUNDING

California's school finance system is highly centralized; state aid accounts for 58 percent of school district revenue (Lincoln Institute and GWIPP 2022; NAEP 2021; NCES 2020, 2021a, 2021b). But California's centralization of school finance is even greater than state-aid statistics suggest. Before 1979, school districts raised more than half their revenue locally and exercised control over their budgets and property tax rates. School finance litigation that began in the early 1970s drove legislation that eroded local control and, in an attempt to equalize school district revenues, gave the state authority to distribute property tax revenues.

Table 4.1

Selected Public School Funding and Performance Data for Case Study States

	United States	California		Massachusetts		South Carolina		Texas		Wisconsin	
Public School Revenue and Spending with Ranks (in green) (FY 2019)											
Local Property Tax Share	39.3%	27.3%	32	51.8%	4	31.8%	21	47.2%	10	39.5%	17
State Share	47.3%	58.0%	13	39.3%	40	49.3%	25	36.6%	45	49.5%	24
Per-Pupil Spending	$13,187	$14,035	18	$17,748	7	$11,140	35	$9,827	44	$12,598	25
Property Tax Features (2019)											
Assessment Limit	32 States	Yes		No		Yes		Yes		No	
Rate or Levy Limit	45 States	Yes		Yes		Yes		Yes		Yes	
Circuit Breaker	34 States	No		Yes		No		No		Yes	
Demographics with Ranks (in green)											
Percent White (Public School Students), Fall 2020	45.8%	21.7%	48	56.8%	25	48.8%	31	26.5%	47	68.4%	14
Percent Black (Public School Students), Fall 2020	15.0%	5.2%	35	9.3%	27	32.6%	6	12.7%	22	8.9%	28
Percent Hispanic (Public School Students), Fall 2020	28.0%	55.4%	2	22.3%	15	11.4%	35	52.9%	3	12.8%	32
School-Age Children Living in Poverty (2019)	15.8%	15.2%	3	11.0%	42	18.7%	8	18.0%	13	12.7%	32
Graduation Rates with Ranks (in green) (FY 2019)											
Cohort Graduation Rate	85.3	84.5	31	88.0	15	81.1	42	90.0	8	90.1	7
NAEP Percent Scoring at or Above Proficient with Ranks (in green) (2019)											
4th Grade Reading	34.3	32.1	38	45.4	1	31.8	39	30.3	46	35.5	21
4th Grade Math	40.4	33.6	46	50.2	2	36.3	41	43.7	16	44.8	13
8th Grade Reading	32.4	29.8	38	44.6	1	29.3	40	25.0	48	38.5	5
8th Grade Math	32.9	28.5	42	47.4	1	28.9	41	29.6	36	41.3	4
NAEP Average Scores by Race/Ethnicity with Race/Ethnicity Gaps (in blue) (gap between average score for white students and other group), 4th Grade Math (FY 2019)											
White Average Score	249	250		254		249		254		249	
Black Average Score	224	25	224	26	232	22	220	29	233	21	212	37
Hispanic Average Score	231	18	225	25	232	22	230	19	238	16	228	22

Note: Race/Ethnicity gaps are subject to rounding errors.

Source: NCES (2021a, 2021b, and 2020); NAEP (2021); Lincoln Institute and GWIPP (2022)

EQUITY LITIGATION: *SERRANO V. PRIEST*

In 1971, the California Supreme Court in *Serrano v. Priest*, 5 Cal.3d 584, 487 P.2d 1241 (1971) (*Serrano I*), concluded that the disparities in property wealth among school districts created by heavy dependence on local property taxes discriminated against the poor and violated California's equal protection clause.

In the wake of *Serrano I*, the legislature enacted Senate Bill 90 in 1972. The legislation increased state foundation formula aid to schools and increased property tax exemptions. Low-wealth districts saw the largest increases in state aid. To offset the cost of the restructuring, the state raised the sales and corporate tax rates (Sonstelie, Brunner, and Ardon 2000). To close the disparities between high- and low-spending districts, SB 90 limited the growth in the sum of state aid (excluding categorical aid) and property tax revenue (a funding component referred to as revenue limits) to no more than 3 percent for the highest-spending districts and 15 percent for the lowest-spending districts. The law permitted districts to override the revenue limits by a simple majority, though fewer than 40 percent of override referenda succeeded in the following two years (Sonstelie, Brunner, and Ardon 2000). Revenue limit funding remained a component of California school finance until 2013.

Five years after its first ruling in *Serrano I*, the California Supreme Court considered the school finance system again, taking into account the SB 90 reforms. In *Serrano v. Priest*, 18 Cal.3d 728, 5557 P.2d 929 (1976) (*Serrano II*), the court found that "the changes . . . , while significant, did not purport to alter the basic concept underlying the California public school financing system." Finding that "substantial disparities in expenditures per pupil resulting from differences in local taxable wealth will continue to exist," the court set out some possible alternative funding methods, including full state funding by statewide property tax and a guaranteed tax base

formula. The California Supreme Court upheld the trial court's order that the legislature reduce wealth-based disparities in combined state and local revenue for school districts to less than $100 per pupil by 1980 (Brunner and Sonstelie 2006; Fischel 1989).

Act 65 of 1977 was the legislature's response to *Serrano II*. The legislation established a guaranteed tax base formula aimed at equalizing the override revenues a school district could raise above the revenue limit (Brunner and Sonstelie 2006). But before Act 65 took effect, voters approved Proposition 13, forestalling power equalization and clinching the centralization of school finance.

TAX REVOLT AND PROPOSITION 13

Proposition 13 was the product of a revolt by property taxpayers whose property tax bills were soaring because of escalating home values in the 1970s without downward adjustment of tax rates (Youngman 2016).

The constitutional amendment enacted by Proposition 13 in 1978 fundamentally altered the property tax by:

- resetting assessed values to the full cash value on the FY 1975–1976 assessment rolls and instituting acquisition value assessment under which properties are reassessed only when sold;
- limiting growth in assessed values to 2 percent per year;
- capping cumulative property tax rates at 1 percent of assessed value;
- eliminating tax limit overrides;
- requiring a two-thirds majority vote by both houses of the California legislature to increase any state tax; and
- requiring a two-thirds majority vote of the electorate for local governments to impose special taxes.

Weeks after Californians adopted Proposition 13, the legislature enacted Senate Bill 154 to allocate property tax revenue among school districts, counties, cities, and special districts according to pre–Proposition 13 levels and to provide state aid to make up for some of the Proposition 13 property tax loss. A year later, the state passed permanent bailout legislation. Assembly Bill 8 of 1979 established a formula for local property tax allocation that, in practice, shifted a portion of school districts' local property tax base to other local governments and backfilled that revenue from the state general fund.

GOALS, OUTCOMES, UNINTENDED CONSEQUENCES, AND REFORMS

The *Serrano* litigation, with its equity goals, and Proposition 13, with its property tax reduction goals,

converged in 1978. The result was a sort of school finance role reversal. As the legislature worked to reduce disparities in funding among school districts to comply with *Serrano II*, Proposition 13 thrust upon the state the authority and responsibility to equitably distribute severely constrained local property tax revenue among the state's local governments and school districts. In 1978, school district tax collections accounted for 50 percent of school district revenue; in 1979 they made up only a quarter of total revenue. State aid, supported mostly by state income taxes, climbed from 36 percent in 1978 to 58 percent in 1979 (U.S. Census Bureau 1978–1979). The ratio of state aid to school district tax collections has averaged 2.7 to 1 since 1979, and fluctuations in the ratio often reflect changing state policies on allocation of funding among local governments (figure 4.1).

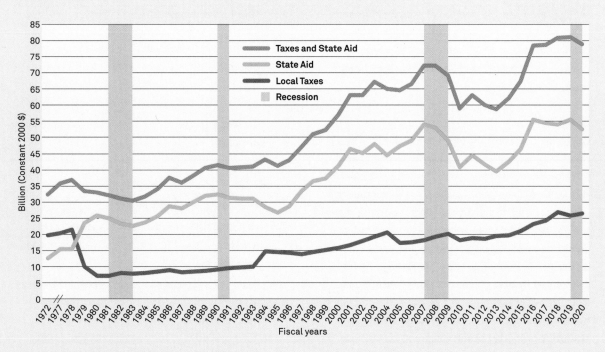

Figure 4.1

California School District Revenue Sources, Selected Years 1972–2020

Sources: U.S. Census Bureau (1972, 1977–1991, 1992–2020)

Schools in California, like San Francisco's Garfield Elementary School, get most funding from the state; less than a third of funding for K–12 education comes from local property taxes. *Source: Anouchka/Getty Images*

In *Serrano v. Priest*, 226 Cal. Rptr. 584 (Court of Appeal, 2d District) (1986) (*Serrano III*), a California court of appeal held that the state's centralized school finance system complied with the state constitution. The court found that 93 percent of California students were in districts with wealth-related spending differences of less than $100 per pupil as mandated by *Serrano II*. Although the reforms satisfied the courts, closing the gaps among school districts in per-pupil spending has not equalized educational outcomes.

By any measure, Proposition 13 achieved its goals to reduce and stabilize property taxes. In the wake of Proposition 13, property tax revenue plummeted, declining 57 percent in the year following passage (Sonstelie, Brunner, and Ardon 2000). But Proposition 13 gave the state full control over school district tax rates, budgets, and distribution of property taxes among local governments and school districts, stripping school districts of control over locally raised property tax revenue. It diminished the role of the property tax, shifting reliance toward state aid supported by state income and sales taxes. Although Proposition 13 brought stability and predictability to assessments and property tax bills, it created inequities, inhibited mobility, and distorted housing markets. As a result of capped assessments and tax rates, owners of similar homes with similar means can face vastly different tax bills. This horizontal inequity led to unsuccessful attempts to overturn acquisition value assessment in the courts in the 15 years after the initiative passed.

Notably, in 1992, the U.S. Supreme Court upheld the constitutionality of acquisition value assessment and the resulting disparities in assessed values of similar properties in *Nordlinger v. Hahn*, 505 U.S. 1, 112 S.Ct. 2326. 120 L.Ed.2d 1 (1992). Although recognizing that, "over time, the acquisition-value system has created dramatic disparities in the taxes paid by persons owning similar pieces of property," the Court found that the scheme furthered neighborhood preservation, continuity, stability, and the interest of the owner who "does not have the option of deciding not to buy his home if taxes become prohibitively high."

Reassessment upon transfer creates a strong incentive for taxpayers to remain in their homes, and it contributes to the state's housing affordability crisis. The system favors longtime homeowners, giving older taxpayers an advantage over younger residents. Since the 1980s, voters have approved portability measures. Portability, which allows taxpayers to transfer their reduced assessment to a new property under certain circumstances, only compounds these inequities.

Brunner and Sonstelie (2006) found that academic achievement levels declined after Proposition 13 and that California's test scores continue to lag behind the rest of the nation's. California students have continued to perform below the national average, although the gaps have narrowed since 2013 (NAEP 2021). However, gaps in scores between Black students and white students in California have not narrowed and remain wider than the national average (table 4.1, page 34).

Downes and Shoeman (1998) suggest that the rapid growth in private school enrollment and decline in public school enrollment after passage of Proposition 13 were partly attributable to the reforms.

In 1977, California spent 18 percent more per pupil than the national average (figure 4.2). In the aftermath of Proposition 13, California's per-pupil spending declined markedly. By 1978, per-pupil spending had slowed relative to that of other states, and it fell below the U.S. average by the 1990s (Sonstelie 2014). Even the minimum education funding mandated by Proposition 98, passed in 1988, did not bring it up to the U.S. average. The measure required the state to expend at least 40 percent of its general fund budget on K–14 education and make guaranteed annual year-over-year adjustments linked to economic and enrollment growth. Education spending increased

following the Local Control Funding Formula reforms in 2013, and it reached the U.S. average in FY 2017–2018, as shown in figure 4.2. Average or below-average spending and high educational costs have left California with the nation's highest pupil-teacher ratio (NCES 2021a; Rueben, Auxier, and Gordon 2020).

The Local Control Funding Formula does away with revenue limits, general-purpose block grants, and most categorical aid programs. The new system establishes per-pupil base grants that vary by grade level, with supplemental grants for English-language learners, students eligible for free and reduced-price meals, and foster youth. The formula targets aid to high-need districts through concentration grants and gives districts more discretion in spending state funds (California Department of Education 2021; Lincoln Institute of Land Policy 2022).

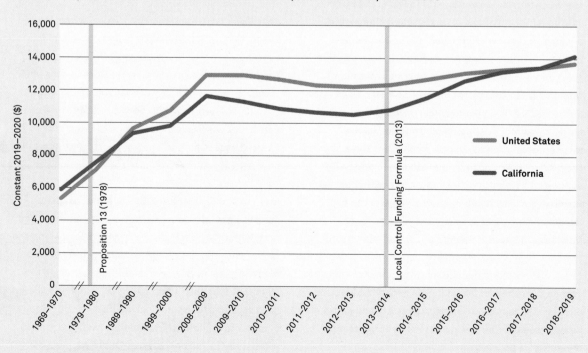

Figure 4.2

Per-Pupil Expenditures, California and United States, Selected Years, 1970–2018

Source: NCES (2021a)

ATTEMPTS TO WORK AROUND OR DISMANTLE PROPOSITION 13

Having lost control over their primary revenue source, school districts and local governments seek other sources. Cities and counties have replaced property tax revenue with sales, hotel, and utility taxes, but school districts still lack broad revenue-raising authority. For California school districts, the parcel tax is "the only real source of discretionary revenue," distinguishable from the property tax because it is not based on value (Sonstelie 2014). Most school district parcel taxes are a flat per-parcel levy—the average school district parcel tax was $134 in 2012. Found only in California, parcel taxes are subject to Proposition 13's required two-thirds approval but are not subject to the property tax limitations and do not reduce state aid (Sonstelie 2014). Only 12 percent of school districts have adopted parcel taxes, and usage is concentrated in the San Francisco Bay Area (Lee 2020).

Though Proposition 13 remains popular with most taxpayers, persistent efforts to amend the state constitution to eliminate acquisition value assessment for nonresidential property show a long-term dissatisfaction with Proposition 13 among some Californians. Such proposals are often debated but rarely make it to the ballot. Voters rejected a measure that made it to the ballot in 1992 and narrowly defeated another, Proposition 15, in November 2020 (California Secretary of State 2020). The 2020 measure, referred to as a split roll property tax, would have returned certain commercial and industrial real property to market value assessment while preserving acquisition value assessment for residential properties and most small businesses (Ballotpedia, n.d.). Proposition 15's failure illustrates the political difficulty of dismantling the Proposition 13 assessment limit.

Massachusetts taxpayers, including Charlie Simas of Arlington, can override the Proposition 2½ tax limits with a majority vote.
Source: Media News Group/Boston Herald via Getty Images

Massachusetts: Successful Property Tax and School Finance Reform

In many ways, Massachusetts serves as a model for how to manage the property tax–school funding dilemma. Inspired in part by California's Proposition 13, Massachusetts had its own property tax revolt, Proposition 2½, enacted in 1982. But Massachusetts's proposition did not include an assessment limit, was not a constitutional amendment, and was subsequently modified by the state legislature to add local government flexibility. It even was used to help reform the state's property tax system.

The Massachusetts Education Reform Act of 1993 was a positive turning point in the state's policy for financing schools. The act targeted state aid to

Massachusetts cut state aid during the Great Recession when the housing crisis led to widespread foreclosures, as in this Boston neighborhood. *Source: REUTERS/Alamy Stock Photo*

the school districts that needed it most and linked accountability standards to increased school aid, producing strong academic results. However, the years since the act's passage show that even strong school finance systems can backslide and should be occasionally reevaluated.

Massachusetts is a high-income state with a strong economy and highly educated population. It ranks seventh among the states in per-pupil spending on K–12 education (table 4.1, page 34). Although its population is growing more slowly than the U.S. average, it is the fastest-growing state in New England. As with many New England states, Massachusetts relies heavily on the property tax, which provides more than half of K–12 funding. Local government is important in Massachusetts, which has 351 cities and towns. K–12 schools are part of city and town governments and not independent governments, as in most states.

A LONG ROAD TO PROPERTY TAX REFORM

In the 1970s, the property tax system was in bad shape: properties were assessed at far less than market value, in what is known as a fractional assessment system. Assessments were infrequently updated, and some properties had not been reassessed since before World War II. Given the low assessments, high tax rates were required to generate sufficient revenue. Even worse, gross inequities existed in effective tax rates: prosperous areas were assessed at low value relative to market value and low-income areas at higher value (Case, Malme, and Rakow, n.d.; Farmer 2021). Despite all these issues, the state heavily relied on the property tax.

The first step in reforming the property tax system was a ruling by the Massachusetts Supreme Court, *Town of Sudbury v. Commissioner of Corporations and Taxation*, 366 Mass. 558, 321 N.E.2d 641 (1974), that the state had the power to require local assessors to value property at full market value. For many years, assessors in Massachusetts had followed an unofficial policy and assessed residential properties at a lower percentage of market value than business properties. If, as required by the court, all property was assessed at 100 percent of market value, a significant part of the property tax burden would shift from business to residential property. In 1978, to avoid such a shift, an amendment to the state's constitution was ratified, permitting differential taxation of four classes of property: residential, open space, commercial, and industrial. Unlike policies in other states, classification became a local option. In the 1979 classification amendment, the legislature prohibited cities or towns from adopting classification unless properties were assessed at full market value.

Massachusetts voters in 1980 approved Proposition 2½, which specified that property taxes could not exceed 2.5 percent of each municipality's assessed value and that property tax levies could not increase by more than 2.5 percent per year. By defining the tax rate limit in terms of the assessed value of property, Proposition 2½ created an additional incentive for municipalities to move to assessments at full market value. By 1986 all municipalities in the state had done so (Case, Malme, and Rakow, n.d.).

DODGING A TAX LIMITATION BULLET

The rate and levy limits imposed by Proposition 2½ had their intended effect of reducing property tax burdens. Before 1980, the ratio of property tax to personal income in Massachusetts was about 75 percent greater than the national average. After the implementation of Proposition 2½, the average property tax burden exceeded the national average by only 20 percent (Urban-Brookings Tax Policy Center, n.d.).

Reducing reliance on the property tax in a state that does not allow local governments to levy either sales or income taxes could easily lead to constrained local government revenues. In this respect, the timing of the enactment of Proposition 2½ was lucky. It came at the beginning of the "Massachusetts Miracle," a period of significant economic growth that enabled the state to increase aid to localities and cushioned the tax limitation's impact.

In many states, tax limitations are constitutional amendments. Proposition 2½, however, is a statute, subject to modification by the legislature. In the years after its passage, the legislature exempted net new construction from the levy limit. In subsequent legislation, the number of voters needed to pass a referendum overriding the 2.5 percent levy limit was reduced from a supermajority to a simple majority.

Reducing reliance on the property tax in a state that does not allow local governments to levy either sales or income taxes could easily lead to constrained local government revenues.

In sum, Proposition 2½ had a significant effect on municipal finances but a smaller effect than its supporters had hoped for or its detractors had feared. Although low-income communities are less likely to both initiate override referenda that raise property tax limits and successfully pass them, Proposition 2½ has proven less restrictive than many property tax limits in other states (Wen et al. 2018). A key feature of Massachusetts's property tax limitation is that it is "a tax restriction built on a system of accurate assessments" (Youngman 2016, 214). Without an assessment limit, assessed values are accurate estimates of the market value of property, and the property tax system is fairer than in states, like California, that have adopted an assessment limit.

SCHOOL FINANCE REFORM'S GRAND BARGAIN: MORE AID PAIRED WITH STANDARDS AND ACCOUNTABILITY

As the state was coming out of a deep recession in the early 1990s, dissatisfaction with the quality of the state's public schools was widespread. The Massachusetts Business Alliance for Education published *Every Child a Winner!* in 1991, calling for "high standards, accountability for performance, and equitable distribution of resources among school districts" (Massachusetts Business Alliance for Education 1991). The state's highest court was considering an equity lawsuit that had been filed in 1978, and the State Board of Education published a report highlighting some school shortcomings (Chester 2014).

In 1993, the legislature passed the Massachusetts Education Reform Act, and the state's highest court ruled in *McDuffy v. Secretary of the Executive Office of Education* that the state was not meeting its constitutional duty to provide an adequate education to all students. Close observers of state politics believe that the threat of *McDuffy* helped prompt the legislature to pass the education reform act. The act mandated a large increase in state aid for education (from $1.6 billion in 1993 to $4 billion in 2002) and a new school funding formula, known as Chapter 70 aid, that targeted school districts most in need of aid. Other components of the reform act were curriculum standards and accountability for schools and students. In 1998, the Massachusetts Comprehensive Assessment System tests were administered for the first time. Students must pass the test to graduate from high school.

A second school funding lawsuit, *Hancock v. Driscoll*, 443 Mass. 428 (2005), was settled in 2005, when the Massachusetts Supreme Judicial Court "lifted its 1993 finding of Constitutional violation and decisively terminated 27 years of litigation" (Costrell 2006, i). In its key finding, the court declared,

> The public education system we review today . . . is not the public education system reviewed in *McDuffy*. . . . A system mired in failure has given way to one that, although far from perfect, shows a steady trajectory of progress (Costrell 2006, 14).

THE STRUCTURE OF STATE AID TO SCHOOLS

Chapter 70 school aid follows the basic design of foundation aid. The formula determines each school district's minimum spending necessary to provide an adequate education. This so-called foundation budget is derived by multiplying the number of students in each of 13 categories (e.g., preschool, elementary, in-district special education) by 11 different cost categories (e.g., classroom and specialist teachers, administration, pupil services) and totaling the amounts for each district. A wage adjustment factor applied to each of the salary-related costs accounts for wage differences across the state. In FY 2021, the statewide average foundation budget was $12,394 per pupil.

As with all foundation aid programs, state aid makes up the difference between the district's minimum local contribution and its foundation budget.

The minimum local contribution each city and town requires depends both on equalized property valuation and total income, weighted equally. As with all foundation aid programs, state aid makes up the difference between the district's minimum local contribution and its foundation budget. The state offers a minimum amount of aid to each municipality, no matter how wealthy.

CHALLENGES TO CONTINUED PROGRESS

Although the original intention behind the Massachusetts Education Reform Act was to reevaluate and, if needed, regularly revise the state's school funding formula, that did not happen. Furthermore, after several years of growth in state school aid, cuts were made in 2004 and then again in 2009, after the onset of the Great Recession. As figure 4.3 shows, after many years in which state aid as a share of total K–12 education revenues grew, beginning in 2007, that share mostly fell. To make matters worse, "unrestricted state aid to localities fell by 44 percent between fiscal years 2001 and 2015, adjusted for inflation" (Lav and Leachman 2018).

In 2015, the Foundation Budget Review Commission was established to review the state's school aid system (Ouellette 2018). The commission concluded that local governments were bearing a disproportionate share of the cost of educating children and that several elements of the foundation aid program, such as how health insurance costs were taken into account, were outdated.

In 2019, the legislature passed the Student Opportunity Act, which better targeted an additional $1.5 billion in school aid to low-income students. This revised school aid system was designed to be phased in over seven years. In 2020, the state delayed the funding increases because of pandemic-related economic uncertainty, but the legislature fully funded the act for the first time in 2021 (Martin 2021).

Massachusetts's achievement is evident in its NAEP test scores. The state's scores were always good, particularly compared with the national average. But NAEP scores within Massachusetts have also improved over time. For example, in 2000, 30.9 percent of fourth graders scored at or above proficient in math. By 2007, 57.6 percent of fourth graders scored at or above proficient. Although scores have gone up and down since then, in no year did fewer than 50 percent of fourth graders score proficient or above in math. Furthermore, in recent years Massachusetts students have ranked the best in the country on NAEP scores.

Figure 4.3

Massachusetts State and Local K–12 Education Revenues

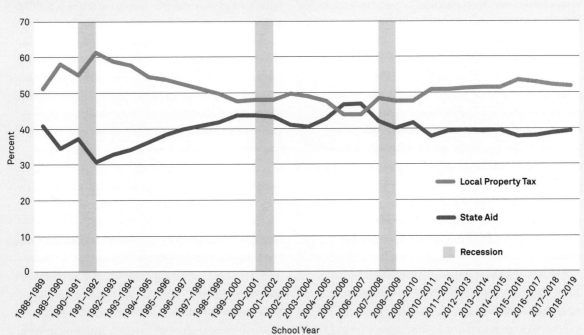

Source: NCES (2021b)

South Carolina exempts homeowners from paying property taxes to support school operating costs. *Source: Image Source/Getty Images*

South Carolina: A Tax Swap and an Outdated School Aid Formula

In 2007, South Carolina implemented Act 388, which fully exempted homeowners from paying local school property taxes on their primary residence in exchange for a one-cent increase in the state sales tax, which was dedicated to public education. South Carolina's local-for-state tax swap was enacted on the eve of the Great Recession, timing that made clear how much less reliable sales taxes are than property taxes in most economic downturns.

South Carolina's state-aid formula is in serious need of updating. For example, the state's measure of school districts' fiscal capacity, the Index of Taxpaying Ability, has not been updated since the tax swap was implemented. South Carolina's experience in recent years demonstrates the possible negative ramifications of property tax limitations on public education.

South Carolina is a relatively low-income but rapidly growing state; its population grew faster than the U.S. average from 2010 to 2019 and is predicted to increase by 21.9 percent from 2010 to 2030 (Urban Institute 2022). About 26 percent of the population is Black, about double the national percentage. All the state's school districts are independent governments, and the number of school districts, about 80 in 2022,

is in flux because of a push to consolidate small rural school districts.

THE TAX SWAP: ACT 388

South Carolina has generous property tax relief for its homeowners. A homestead exemption for all property taxes on the first $50,000 of a residence's value for senior or disabled homeowners was passed in 1972. In 1995, the legislature enacted state-funded property tax relief for homeowners that exempted the first $100,000 of market value of primary residential properties from school-operating property taxes (Saltzman and Ulbrich 2012). At the time, the median value of an owner-occupied home was around $86,500, making many owners completely exempt from school-operating property taxes. Over the next decade, rising property values and school spending put pressure on the legislature to further restructure the property tax system.

In 2006, the legislature passed Act 388, which replaced the school operations tax on primary residential properties with a one-cent increase in the state sales tax. South Carolina thus became, and remains, the only state that fully exempts homeowners from property taxes that help pay to operate public elementary and secondary schools. In addition to this exemption, Act 388 imposed a millage cap and an assessment cap. The millage cap restricted property tax rate growth to inflation plus population growth. The assessment cap was passed by constitutional amendment, limiting growth in the assessed value of property to 15 percent over any five-year period. However, the limit on assessment growth does not apply to properties that are sold—those are reassessed at their full market value.

Act 388 increased reliance on the sales tax, which is a less stable source of revenue than the property tax. The revenue from the sales tax rate increase was earmarked for the Homestead Exemption Fund, which funds schools. The state anticipated an $84 million increase in sales tax revenue in the first year of implementation. Unfortunately, 2007 was the first year of the Great Recession, and instead of increasing, annual sales tax revenues decreased by 11.7 percent from 2007 to 2008 and by 8.7 percent from 2008 to 2009 (Ullrich 2013).

The state promised to maintain the same amount of school funding for the 2007–2008 school year as the previous year through a dollar-for-dollar reimbursement to school districts (Ullrich 2013). Act 388 specified that the fund to reimburse school districts for lost property tax revenues would grow annually at a rate equal to inflation plus population growth. The reimbursements would be allocated based on school districts' share of weighted pupils. The decline in sales tax revenues during the Great Recession and sluggish growth thereafter forced the state to partially fund reimbursements from the state's general fund in every year until FY 2020–2021. In 2009–2010 alone, $116 million of general fund revenue went to helping finance the Homestead Exemption Fund (South Carolina Revenue and Fiscal Affairs Office 2022). Figure 4.4 illustrates the financing of the Homestead Exemption Fund through 2020–2021.

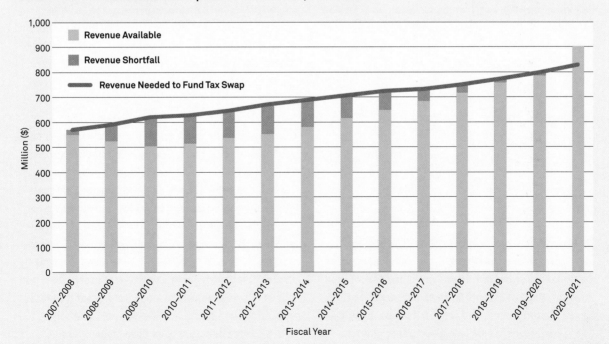

Figure 4.4

South Carolina Homestead Exemption Fund Revenue, 2007–2021

Sources: South Carolina Revenue and Fiscal Affairs Office (2022)

Although the state agreed to fully compensate school districts for property tax revenue lost to the expanded homestead exemption, it made no promises regarding existing state aid. In 2008–2009, the state cut other school funding by $365 million (Salazar and Saltzman 2013). State governments often reduce aid during economic downturns, but the severity of the Great Recession made the cut in state aid especially deep.

THE STRUCTURE OF STATE AID TO SCHOOLS

State aid to school districts has three major components. One is school district reimbursement for property tax relief to homeowners. School districts are partially reimbursed for the property tax relief acts passed in 1972 and 1995 and Act 388's homestead exemption. Reimbursement for school districts under the 1972 property tax relief act was capped in total and for each school district by Act 388. Total reimbursement for school districts is now $81 million. Reimbursement for the 1995 property tax relief act has been capped in total and for each school district since 2001–2002. Total reimbursement is now $249 million. Reimbursement for Act 388's property tax relief totaled approximately $829 million in 2020–2021 (South Carolina Revenue and Fiscal Affairs Office 2022).

State governments often reduce aid during economic downturns, but the severity of the Great Recession made the cut in state aid especially deep.

The Education Finance Act of 1977, a type of foundation program, is the second major component of state aid. The state pays 70 percent of the cost of the program, and local school districts pay 30 percent. A school district's number of weighted pupils multiplied by the base student cost multiplied by the district's Index of Taxpaying Ability determines the amount received. For example, a student with special needs receives a weight greater than one. In 2020–2021, base student cost was $2,489 unweighted. The Index of Taxpaying Ability is a measure of the school district's property tax wealth compared with that of other districts (one measure of fiscal capacity). The higher the index for a school district, the less funding it receives. This index has not been revised since Act 388 exempted owner-occupied homes, so it overstates the fiscal capacity of districts with a high proportion of owner-occupied homes.

The final component of state aid to school districts is its many categorical aid programs.

South Carolina has used the same basic foundation aid formula for more than 40 years, though intermittent efforts are made to reform the system. In 2019, Governor Henry McMaster asked the South Carolina Office of Revenue and Fiscal Affairs to devise a new education funding model. When the new model was shown to create both losers and winners, the plan went nowhere (Adcox 2019). After the pandemic began in March 2020, the near-term prospects for school reform were further reduced as the legislature grappled with pandemic-related issues and uncertain economic forecasts.

SCHOOL FINANCE LAWSUITS

South Carolina has a long series of state supreme court rulings over school finance known as *Abbeville v. State*. First filed by 40 rural school districts in 1993, then amended in 1995, *Abbeville v. State* charged that the state's school finance system violated the state's education clause, the equal protection clauses of the state and federal constitutions, and the Education Finance Act (Allen 2018). In 1999, the South Carolina Supreme Court upheld the plaintiffs' claim that the state was not providing an adequate education, ruling that the state's education clause "requires the General Assembly to provide the opportunity for each child to receive a minimally adequate education" (*Abbeville County School District v. State*, 515 S.E.2d 535 [S.C. 1999]).

Eventually, in 2014, the South Carolina Supreme Court in a 3–2 decision found that the state was not providing a minimally adequate education to all its students. The court imposed no specific remedies but asked the plaintiffs and defendant to present a plan to address the constitutional violations (*Abbeville v. State*, 410 S.C. 619, 767 S.E.2d 157 [2014]).

In subsequent years, the supreme court issued orders, and various reports were submitted to the court.

South Carolina has grown faster than most states since 2010, and growth is expected to continue in the 2020s. *Source: Mark Castiglia/iStock/Getty Images Plus*

The chief justice who had issued the 2014 *Abbeville* decision retired, and the legislature appointed a new justice to the state's highest court. In 2017, the South Carolina Supreme Court reversed itself and in a 3–2 decision ruled that the 2014 decision had been "wrongly decided as violative of separation of powers." The dissenting opinion stated, "Unfortunately, our Court has lost the will to do even the minimal amount necessary to avoid becoming complicit actors in the deprivation of a minimally adequate education to South Carolina's students" (SchoolFunding.Info 2021).

HAS ACT 388 LED TO INADEQUATE SCHOOL FUNDING?

Because of the assessment cap and millage cap imposed by Act 388 in 2007, real per-pupil property tax revenue growth flattened. It grew at an average rate

of 3.3 percent per year from 1993–1994 to 2006–2007, compared with 0.5 percent from 2006–2007 to 2019–2020 (figure 4.5). The rate of growth of state and federal real per-pupil revenue also slowed during the same period.

Slowing growth in real per-pupil revenue could plausibly lead to school spending lower than desired or necessary for providing an adequate education. Anderson (2020) examined 20 school districts in South Carolina from 10 counties chosen as representative of the state as a whole. He found that a majority of the school districts experienced slower growth in instructional expenditure per pupil after Act 388. He also found that school districts in fast-growing counties were more likely to have slower per-pupil revenue growth after Act 388. This may explain some of the interest in and adoption of impact fees by South Carolina school districts in the years since Act 388 (Slade 2020). Impact fees are one-time payments imposed on developers to offset the financial effect of new development, including school costs.

Given the obvious link between revenue and expenditures and the extensive literature establishing a direct relationship between expenditure per pupil and student achievement (see chapter 1, "Money Matters"), there is little question that Act 388 has negatively affected student achievement in at least some South Carolina school districts. South Carolina students have consistently scored well below the national average on the NAEP fourth- and eighth-grade math and reading exams (table 4.1, page 34). Student performance on the reading exams improved between 2007 and 2019, but performance on the eighth-grade math exams worsened.

Figure 4.5

South Carolina Real Per-Pupil Revenue by Source, 1993–1994 to 2019–2020

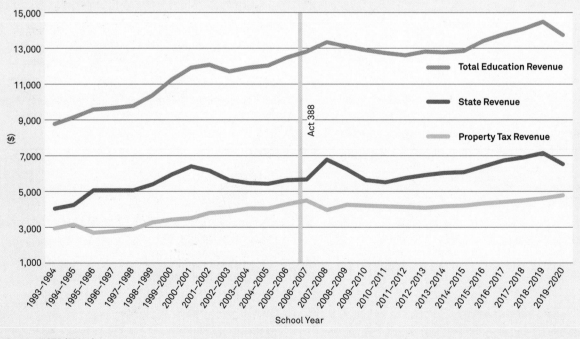

Source: NCES (2021a)

Texas: The Courts' and the Legislature's Search for School Finance Reform

This San Antonio classroom shows the diversity of the student population in Texas, where more than half is Hispanic. *Source: Yellow Dog Productions/Photodisc/Getty Images*

Texas relies more heavily on the property tax to fund state and local government than all but a handful of states. Homeowner property tax burdens are high, and the state's failure to adjust its foundation formula for rising costs and rising property values has led to periodic increases in the share of school funding from the property tax and its higher burden on homeowners. Property tax relief in Texas has been untargeted, and the state does not employ a property tax circuit breaker.

The long history of school funding litigation in Texas has challenged the state to devise a system that provides equitable educational opportunities to all Texas public school students. The legislature has responded by developing a system of state aid that combines a foundation formula with a guaranteed tax base formula and revenue limits on wealthy districts. Its state-aid system also accounts for a range of student and school district characteristics that raise the costs of providing students an adequate education.

Texas educates 5.5 million students in its public schools, nearly 11 percent of all public school students

in the United States. It is a relatively low-spending state with a diverse student body. Operating expenditures per student for the 2018–2019 school year were $9,827, or 25 percent less than the national average (table 4.1, page 34). In 2019–2020, 53 percent of students were Hispanic, 27 percent were white, and 13 percent were Black (Texas Education Agency 2021a). With 1,022 independent school districts, Texas has more school districts than any other state.

THE SEARCH FOR EQUITY THROUGH SCHOOL FUNDING LITIGATION

In *San Antonio Independent School District v. Rodriguez*, 411 U.S. 1, 93 S.Ct. 1278, 36 L.Ed.2d 16 (1973), plaintiffs argued successfully in federal district court that the heavy reliance on local property taxes to fund education denied students in property-poor districts equal rights under the 14th Amendment to the U.S. Constitution. That decision was reversed by the U.S. Supreme Court in a 5–4 decision, which stated that although education is clearly important, it is not a right explicitly guaranteed in the Constitution. Since that ruling, all school funding litigation in Texas and throughout the nation has been based on state constitutional provisions.

The Texas Supreme Court ruled in *Edgewood Independent School District v. Kirby et al.,* 777 S.W.2d 391 (1989) that the state's school funding system was unconstitutional because its heavy reliance on the property tax and large variations among school districts in property wealth led to big differences in school district per-pupil spending.

After several attempts to devise a school funding system that satisfied the Texas Supreme Court, in 1993 the legislature enacted Senate Bill 7, which established a school funding system that met the court's equity standards. The new system, designed to achieve access equality, took a two-tier approach that included a foundation formula and a GTB formula. The legislation also included a provision, Chapter 41, that limited the revenue that could be raised by property-wealthy school districts.

The school funding system is a complex combination of formulas, adjustments, and pupil weights known collectively as the Foundation School Program.

Since the 19th century, the legislature has placed limits on local school property tax rates (Thomas and Walker 1982). At the beginning of the 21st century, the maximum rate for financing maintenance and operations was $1.50 per $100 of assessed value. Plaintiff school districts in *Neeley v. West Orange– Cove Consolidated Independent School District,* 176 S.W.3d 746 (2005) asserted that the pressure to provide students an adequate education and reductions

in state education aid were forcing most school districts to tax at or near the tax rate limit, so they no longer had meaningful control over their tax rates. They argued that the local school property tax had become a de facto state property tax, which is prohibited under the state constitution. The supreme court accepted the plaintiffs' argument and declared the school funding system unconstitutional. In 2006, in response to the supreme court's decision, the legislature enacted House Bill 1, which increased state funding of education and reduced local school property taxes by 14 percent (Texas Education Agency 2021c).

In 2014, the constitutionality of the school funding system was again challenged in court. The plaintiffs' suit returned to the issues addressed in previous school funding cases: the funding inequities created by unequal property tax bases, the inability to provide adequate education because of insufficient state funding, and the lack of discretion in setting local tax rates because of a stringent tax rate cap. In *Morath v. Texas Taxpayer & Student Fairness* Coalition, 490 S.W.3d 826 (2016), the supreme court reversed a lower court decision and ruled that the school funding system, although "undeniably imperfect," was constitutional.

A COMPLEX STATE-AID SYSTEM

The school funding system is a complex combination of formulas, adjustments, and pupil weights known collectively as the Foundation School Program. The largest part of state aid is distributed through a cost-adjusted foundation formula referred to as tier I. The foundation level is the basic allotment and is $6,160. Total tier I foundation support is determined by multiplying the basic allotment by districts' weighted number of pupils. Small districts (fewer than 1,600 pupils) and midsize districts (fewer than 5,000 pupils) receive somewhat higher allotments. As with any foundation formula, tier I aid to a school district is the difference between its total foundation support and the amount of property tax revenue that it can raise

by multiplying the assessed value of its property tax base by a required rate—in this case, $0.92 per $100 of assessed value.

School districts that choose tax rates of more than $0.92 receive additional state aid (referred to as "tier II") allocated using a two-level GTB formula. The first level of tier II provides additional state aid for each one-cent increase in local school property tax rates, up to $1.00. School districts with lower property values receive more aid. The second level of tier II targets aid to low-property-wealth school districts that choose tax rates between $1.00 and $1.07.

In school year 2019–2020, school district property wealth per student ranged from about $41,200 to $141 million (Texas Education Agency 2021b). Because high-property-value school districts could realize higher per-pupil revenues from the property tax than the per-pupil revenues supported by the state-aid formulas, the Foundation School Program includes a recapture provision under which the state takes excess revenue generated by high-property-wealth districts and redistributes it to districts with lower property wealth.

Texas students celebrate their graduation from Spring High School in Harris County. *Source: Paola Garcia Broeders/ Dreamstime.com*

SCHOOL FUNDING POLICY DETERMINES THE ROLE OF THE PROPERTY TAX IN FINANCING EDUCATION

In the tier I foundation formula, any increase in property values will increase the property tax share of tier I funding, because the state's Foundation School Program funding is contingent on local school districts levying property taxes at the required $0.92 rate. Only if the legislature increases the basic or other allotments or lowers the required local tax rate will the share of local funding be reduced.

Figure 4.6 (page 53) illustrates the share of total public education revenue from the local property tax between school years 1988–1989 and 2018–2019 for Texas and for the average of all 50 states and the District of Columbia. Over the 30-year period covered in the graph, on average the property tax accounted for 35 percent of total education revenue in the United States and 43 percent in Texas. During this period, the property tax share in Texas fluctuated between 39 and 47 percent. Although several factors determine the property tax share, much of the variation over time can be explained by changes in school funding policy.

A large increase in the basic allotment between FY 1990 and FY 1992 led to a decline in the property tax share in FY 1993. An 18 percent increase in state aid in FY 1996 and FY 1998 led to declines in the property tax share in the late 1990s. The period of no change in the basic allotment between FY 2000 and FY 2006, coupled with rising property values, led to a sharp rise in the property tax share of total education funding. In FY 2006 and FY 2007, in response to the supreme court's *West Orange-Cove* ruling, school millage rates were lowered, and in FY 2007 and FY 2008, the legislature enacted large increases in state education aid. That caused a sharp drop in the role of property taxes in the funding of education. The property tax share then rose through FY 2019, except for FY 2009 to FY 2011, when another increase in the basic allotment and the federal stimulus payments lowered the property tax share of revenue.

The legislature could prevent future increases in the share of school funding coming from the property tax by annually adjusting the tier I foundation formula for inflation and for any increases in the costs of per-pupil education.

2019 REFORMS TOOK PLACE WITHOUT LITIGATION

In 2019, the legislature enacted major changes to the state's school funding and property tax systems, spurred by two developments. After being quite stable for years, housing prices in Texas started to climb in 2012 (Saving 2018). Although total education funding per pupil remained largely unchanged between 2016 and 2019, due to rising property values, the state's share of the Foundation School Program fell from

43.7 to 35.9 percent, with a corresponding rise in the local government share (Texas Legislative Budget Board 2020).

Rising home values combined with the increased role of the property tax in funding public education resulted in rising property tax burdens on homeowners. In figure 4.7, property tax burdens on homeowners are measured as the median property tax paid by homeowners relative to their median household incomes. Property tax burdens not only are higher in Texas than the national average, but they have been rising faster than in the rest of the country since 2014.

Texas provides property tax relief in large part by reducing school property tax rates.

Texas provides property tax relief in large part by reducing school property tax rates. These mandated rate reductions cut property taxes for all property owners, rather than targeting relief to homeowners. Although local school districts give homeowners property tax exemptions, the state has not enacted circuit breaker legislation, which would give tax relief to homeowners who face particularly high property tax burdens.

House Bill 3, enacted in 2019, changed the school funding system in several important ways. First, it increased the basic allotment by $1,020 per pupil, the first increase since 2016. Second, it increased the per-pupil weights for students receiving special education, bilingual education, and compensatory education, and it supported full-time pre–K education with new funding. Third, it mandated reductions in school property tax rates by reducing the foundation formula property tax rate by eight cents, with the lost revenue to be made up through increased state funding. Additional state aid was provided by increasing the GTB in the first level of tier II aid, although any tax rate increase now requires unanimous school board approval and voter approval.

Figure 4.6

Texas and U.S. Property Tax Revenue as Percentage of Total Public Education Revenue, 1989–2019

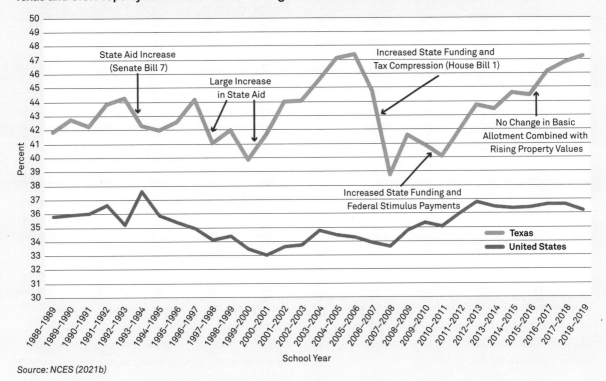

Source: NCES (2021b)

Figure 4.7

Texas and U.S. Median Real Estate Tax Paid by Homeowners as a Percentage of Median Household Income of Homeowners, 2010–2019

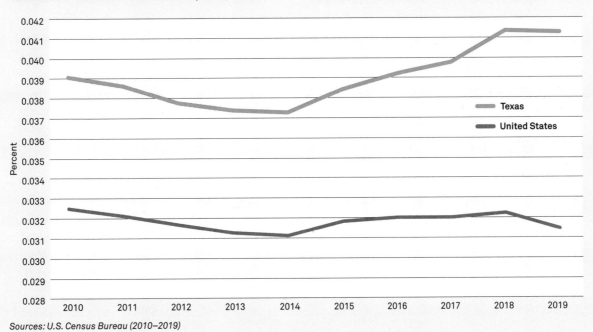

Sources: U.S. Census Bureau (2010–2019)

CHALLENGES AHEAD

In addition to the school funding challenges faced by most states, Texas has unique demographic challenges. Texas is a rapidly growing state. According to enrollment projections by the National Center for Education Statistics (Hussar and Bailey 2020), by 2028 public school enrollment in Texas will be 5.6 percent higher than in 2020. In the rest of the country, 2028 enrollment is projected to grow by only 0.6 percent, and it will decline in 18 states.

With growing enrollments come increased costs. The proportion of students from poor families has risen: 56.6 percent of students were classified as economically disadvantaged in 2008–2009. By the 2019–2020 school year, that number was 60.3 percent (Texas Education Agency 2021a). Predicting future trends is difficult, but the costs of public education in Texas are likely to rise even faster than the growth of the student population.

Texas also must contend with how to improve the quality of education its students receive. The state has a mixed record on student performance. On both the fourth- and eighth-grade NAEP reading exams, students in Texas perform below the national average (table 4.1, page 34). These low reading scores reflect in part the heavy concentration of Hispanic students. One bright spot is the fourth-grade mathematics exam, on which Texas students exceed the national average. By the eighth grade, however, their math scores fell below the national average (NAEP, 2021). Texas has made considerable efforts to improve the quality of its education system by developing a sophisticated accountability system. It has also encouraged its school districts to operate as efficiently and effectively as possible. Improving student performance may need to include a commitment to increase per-student spending.

Wisconsin: School Funding Decisions Motivated by Efforts to Reduce School Property Taxes

Since at least the 1980s, legislative debates about public school funding have been animated by two competing goals: ensuring that all schools have sufficient revenues to provide students a high-quality education and reducing school property taxes. Despite some progress toward both goals, improvements in student academic achievement have stagnated, racial gaps in educational performance are extraordinarily large, and the share of public school revenues coming from the property tax remains above the national average.

School funding in Wisconsin is intertwined with ongoing efforts to reduce property taxes. State-imposed revenue caps that mandate property tax rate reductions limit school districts' ability to use state equalization aid to increase education spending. In contrast to most states, Wisconsin does not account for differences in the spending needs of school districts in its equalization aid formula, which likely contributes to the large differences in the academic performance of students characterized by race and household income.

Wisconsin has 421 independent school districts; half the revenue used to fund them in FY 2019 came from the state government and 40 percent came from the local property tax (table 4.1, page 34).

A HISTORY OF PROPERTY TAX LIMITATIONS IN THE GUISE OF SCHOOL FUNDING REFORM

Despite increases in state aid in the 1970s, school property tax levies and per-pupil spending grew rapidly during the 1980s and early 1990s. As illustrated in figure 4.8 (page 56), by school year 1992–1993, property tax revenue accounted for 53 percent of public education revenues. Responding to these spending and property tax increases, the legislature during the 1990s acted to reduce school property taxes.

- Before 1993, salary and benefit disputes with teachers were resolved using mediation and binding arbitration. Because arbitrators often sided with teachers, the legislature in effect capped increases in teacher compensation by limiting the use of mediation and arbitration.

- To help enforce property tax reductions, the legislature restricted how much school districts could raise from the sum of equalization aid and property taxes starting in the 1993–1994 school year. The annual per-pupil increase in these revenue limits was initially set at $190. For the next 15 years, this per-pupil adjustment to the revenue limits increased at roughly the rate of inflation. State categorical grants and federal aid are not subject to the revenue limit. Despite these exclusions, more than 80 percent of total school district revenue is subject to the revenue limit. The only way a school district can increase revenues above the annual revenue cap is through an override referendum approved by a majority of local voters.

- To fulfill a commitment to fund two-thirds of the cost of public education, the legislature between school years 1995–1996 and 1996–1997 increased state aid by 32 percent. With more than half the increased state aid going to fund property tax relief, the average K–12 property tax rate declined by 26 percent over the next two years.

Figure 4.8

Wisconsin and U.S. Property Tax Revenue as a Percentage of Total Public Education Revenues

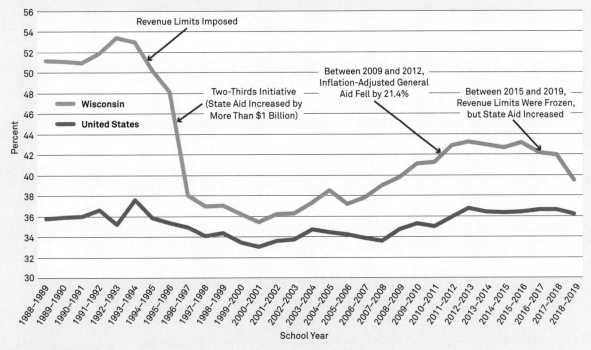

Source: NCES (2021b)

By school year 2000–2001, the combined effect of these policies had reduced the school property tax as a share of total education revenue by nearly 20 percentage points (figure 4.8). Nevertheless, the property tax share remained above the national average.

Figure 4.9 displays the annual allowable increases in revenue limits. In school year 2011–2012, revenue limits were reduced by more than $550 per pupil on average, and later in the decade, they were frozen for four consecutive years. Because revenue limits are defined as the sum of equalization aid and property taxes, whenever a school district's per-pupil aid is increased by more than the annual revenue limit adjustment, every dollar of state aid above the limit must be offset by a dollar-for-dollar reduction in the district's property tax levy.

In 2011, the legislature passed Act 10, which weakened teacher unions and reduced teacher compensation by requiring them to pay a larger share of their health care costs and pension benefits. In the school year 2011–2012, the governor justified a nearly 10 percent budget cut in equalization aid plus the negative revenue limit adjustment by arguing that Act 10 supplied school districts the tools they needed to cut spending.

In recent years, the cumulative effect of the revenue limits has led to an increasing number of successful revenue limit overrides. In FY 2021, 35 percent of school districts passed overrides.

Figure 4.9

Wisconsin Revenue Limit Per-Pupil Adjustments

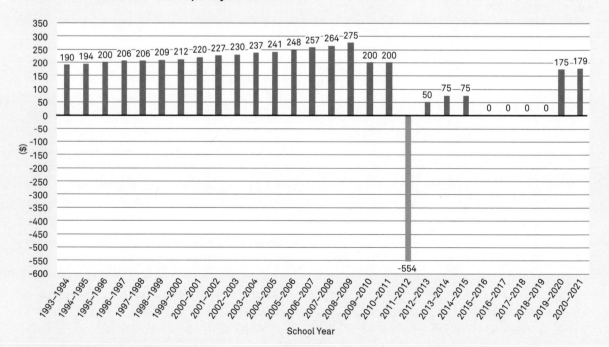

Note: For 2011–12, the revenue limit adjustment was –5.5 percent; the average reduction for school districts was $554 per pupil.

Source: Kava (2021); Kava and Drilias (2019)

MOST PROPERTY TAX RELIEF IS UNTARGETED

Wisconsin provides property tax relief either by targeting property tax reductions to specific groups, such as homeowners, farmers, or low-income households, or by incentivizing or mandating that local governments, including school districts, reduce property tax rates. Lowering property tax rates results in equal percentage tax reductions to all owners of nonagricultural taxable property, including homeowners, owners of commercial-industrial property, and out-of-state owners of vacation homes.

All property owners benefit from the School Levy Credit through reductions in school property tax rates.

The school funding system provides untargeted property tax relief by increasing state equalization aid per pupil by an amount greater than the annual revenue limit adjustment. For example, in FY 2017, the legislature increased general aid by $108.3 million while not allowing any revenue limit increases. As a result, most school districts were forced to reduce their property tax rates to remain under their revenue limits. Several tax credits also offer property tax relief. In FY 2021, credits reduced property taxes by nearly $1.9 billion. Almost 60 percent was from two untargeted credits: the School Levy Credit and the First Dollar Credit.

All property owners benefit from the School Levy Credit through reductions in school property tax rates. The state government then reimburses local school districts for their reduced property tax revenues. In an analysis of the credit, Reschovsky (2010) estimates that 51 percent of the credit was used to reduce the property taxes of Wisconsin homeowners on their

Wisconsin's legislature enacted policies in the 1990s to limit school taxes, restricting school districts' ability to increase spending on education and diminishing the role of the property tax. *Source: YinYang/iStock/Getty Images Plus*

limits unchanged since 2010, the average credit was only $493 in FY 2019.

The combined impact of the revenue limits and property tax credits on Wisconsin homeowners can be assessed by calculating changes in their property tax burdens over time. Using data from the U.S. Census Bureau's (2010–2019) American Community Survey, we estimate tax burdens by dividing the median property tax paid by homeowners by median household income. Between 2010 and 2019, homeowner property tax burdens in Wisconsin fell by about 15 percent but nevertheless remained 35 percent larger than the average homeowner property tax burden in the United States. The tax burden on homeowners remains high partly because Wisconsin relies mainly on untargeted property tax relief.

STATE-AID FORMULAS FAIL TO ADDRESS PERSISTENT EDUCATIONAL ACHIEVEMENT GAPS

Wisconsin students in 2019 performed at about the national average on the NAEP fourth-grade reading exam and above the national average on the fourth-grade math exam and on both eighth-grade exams (see table 4.1, page 34).

The NAEP results are troubling, however, with respect to achievement gaps between white and Black students. The gaps on all four exams were larger in Wisconsin than in any other state; only the District of Columbia had larger gaps. White students perform at the national average, whereas Black students' results are the lowest among all states reporting Black students' scores. Despite recent policy initiatives designed to reduce

primary residences. The remaining credits went to the owners of commercial-industrial property, farmland, and residential rental property and to both Wisconsin and out-of-state owners of vacation properties.

Wisconsin provides additional property tax relief through three tax credits targeted to homeowners. The largest of these is the School Property Tax/Rent Credit, a nonrefundable income tax credit equal to 12 percent of the first $2,500 in property taxes paid on a principal residence. Renters are also eligible for a credit; 25 percent of their rent is considered a property tax payment. The Lottery and Gaming Tax Credit exempts a fixed amount of assessed value of homeowners' primary residences. In FY 2021, the exempted amount was $17,400. The Homestead Credit is a circuit breaker; homeowners and renters receive a refundable income tax credit that rises as their property tax liabilities exceed a fixed percentage of their incomes. Because of income eligibility and other the racial achievement gap, the gaps reported on the 2019 NAEP are larger than those in 2011.

Reasons for the persistent racial and economic achievement gaps are complex. One factor is that Wisconsin's school funding system largely fails to account for the varying funding different school districts need per student to meet state-imposed standards for a high-quality education.

In FY 2021, state aid to local school districts totaled $6.3 billion. Nearly 80 percent of that came from the state's general equalization aid formula. Equalization aid was distributed through a foundation aid formula supplemented by a GTB formula. The highly complex three-tier formula weakens the link between school district per-student property values and the amount of money available to fund education. It also encourages property-poor districts to increase spending and discourages property-rich districts from increasing their spending. The formula reduces aid to many school districts with above-average per-pupil property wealth that choose to increase education spending.

Although the formula does reduce the link between per-pupil property wealth and school district revenue, it takes no account of the resource needs of school districts. Unlike most states, Wisconsin's equalization aid formula does not use pupil weights to adjust for

school districts' differing costs and needs. Wisconsin has more than 30 separate categorical aid programs that are outside the revenue limits and thus can be used to finance additional spending. The single categorical aid grant targeted to low-income students can be used only for educating kindergarten through third-grade students, and funding for this program has not increased since FY 2010. The largest categorical aid is for special education. The aid partially reimburses school districts for spending on federally mandated programs for students with disabilities. Despite a recent increase in special education aid, state and federal aid in FY 2020 covered only 35 percent of the amount school districts spent on special education services. The remainder had to be funded out of general school district revenues.

The most significant change in the state's school funding policy since 2011 was a per-pupil aid program established in FY 2013. Per-pupil aid is outside the revenue limits and, by definition, its distribution is unrelated to the property wealth of school districts or to their expenditure needs. Between its inception in FY 2013 and FY 2021, per capita aid has increased by nearly 40 percent annually. The increase in per-pupil aid brought needed revenue to school districts, but because it is completely untargeted it does nothing to equalize school funding and little to address Wisconsin's racial and economic achievement gaps.

Wisconsin distributes most aid to schools through its general equalization aid formula, which aims to reduce disparities between property-poor and property-wealthy school districts but fails to adjust for differences in student needs and costs. *Source: Hannah Babiak/ Dreamstime.com*

CHAPTER 5

Property Taxes and School Funding in the Case Study States

The goal of this chapter is to assess the school funding systems in the five case study states to help inform the policy recommendations in chapter 6. The first part of this chapter focuses on the property tax systems in each of the case study states, and the second part of the chapter looks at the success and failures of each state in providing adequate and equitable school funding.

Among our case studies, Massachusetts has the best student academic performance and the most progressive state-aid system. (Boston). *Source: Sean Pavone/Getty Images*

Only two of the case study states target property tax relief via circuit breakers—Massachusetts and Wisconsin—and both states' circuit breaker programs fall short of ideal. California and Wisconsin have particularly stringent tax limits that apply to school property taxes.

Massachusetts is one of only nine states in which per-pupil education spending in high-poverty school districts exceeds the amount that Baker et al. (2021) estimate is necessary to provide an adequate education. California, South Carolina, and Texas are among the 28 states where spending in the highest-poverty districts was at least 20 percent less than the estimate for an adequate education. All the case study states fund state aid to K–12 education in a progressive manner, but only California and South Carolina provide sufficiently progressive state aid to counterbalance the regressivity of their local revenue systems so that total state-local funding is progressive.

Evaluating Property Tax Systems

Table 5.1 features two important aspects of property tax systems in the case study states: the use and characteristics of circuit breaker programs (which only exist in two of the states) and the imposition of tax limits on local school districts. As explained in chapter 2, circuit breakers make property tax systems more equitable by reducing property taxes for

Table 5.1

Comparing State Property Tax Systems

Criteria	California	Massachusetts	South Carolina	Texas	Wisconsin
Property Tax Circuit Breakers					
Property Tax Circuit Breaker (CB)?	No	Yes	No	No	Yes
Eligibility		Homeowners and renters, age 65+			Homeowners and renters, age 18+
Maximum CB Benefit		$1,130			$1,168
CB Income Ceiling (Married Couples)		$90,000			$24,680
Tax Limitations					
Property Tax Assessment Limits	Lesser of 2% or rate of inflation	No	15% within a 5-year period	10%	No
Property Tax Rate Limit	1%	2.5%	Rate increases limited to % cost of living + % change in population	No	No
Property Tax Levy Limit	No	2.5%, excluding tax base growth	No	8%	No
Revenue or Expenditure Limit	% cost of living + % change in population	No	No	No	Limit on sum of state aid and property tax revenue

Source: Lincoln Institute (2022), Lincoln Institute of Land Policy and George Washington Institute of Public Policy (GWIPP) (2022)

Spending in Texas' highest poverty school districts is nearly 50 percent below the level analysts estimate would be required to achieve adequacy (Baker et al. 2021). *Source: ssucsy/ Getty Images/iStock Unreleased*

taxpayers whose tax liabilities are particularly high relative to their incomes.

The Massachusetts income eligibility ceiling is quite high—$90,000—but the credit is restricted to the elderly and capped at a modest $1,130. Nonelderly taxpayers, many of whom face high property tax burdens, are unable to benefit from the circuit breaker. Although Wisconsin's circuit breaker is open to all adult households, eligibility is limited to those with incomes less than $24,680, thereby excluding many households with modest incomes. Thus, total circuit breaker credits in Wisconsin in 2018 equaled only 0.8 percent of total property tax revenue.

The different types of tax limits that apply to school property taxes are listed in the second panel of table 5.1. When property tax limits are too stringent, they undercut local fiscal autonomy. They can also make the property tax more complex and less transparent for the taxpayer. By capping both the property tax rate and the rate of growth of assessed values, California's limits have proven quite restrictive. In Massachusetts, because of the rapid growth of property values and the frequent use of overrides to exceed levy limits, they have been only modestly restrictive. The absence of a levy limit or a fixed rate

cap in South Carolina has minimized the restrictiveness of its limits.

Only California and Wisconsin impose limits on school district revenues or expenditures, and those limits are quite restrictive.

Evaluating School Funding Systems

To summarize the strengths and weaknesses of the school funding systems in the five case study states, we use the indicators of adequacy, fiscal effort, and progressivity developed by Baker et al. (2021).

ADEQUACY

Baker et al. (2021) use a statistical model to calculate how much each school district must spend per pupil to achieve a common academic goal. To make interstate comparisons, the student achievement goal the researchers choose is the U.S. average test score results on the NAEP. Drawing on 2019 data from Baker et al. (2021), table 5.2 focuses on educational adequacy in the 20 percent of school districts with the highest concentration of students from poor families. Actual per-pupil spending in those districts is compared with the estimated amount needed for an adequate education. The numbers in the first column indicate that actual spending in California is 26 percent less than adequate spending. California, along with South Carolina and Texas, is among the 28 states where spending in the highest-poverty quintile was at least 20 percent less than the level needed for an adequate education. Massachusetts is one of only nine states where spending in high-poverty districts exceeded the adequacy standard.

FISCAL EFFORT

School funding depends on the size of a state's economy and residents' willingness to use the state's resources. Baker et al. (2021) define fiscal effort to support education as total K–12 education spending by the state and local governments as a percentage of gross state product (GSP), a standard measure of the size of a state's economy. The data on fiscal effort in the five case studies is presented in the second column of table 5.2.

South Carolina exerts the most effort of the five states, suggesting that its poor educational performance is partly due to its relatively small economic base. Only five states have a lower GSP per capita than South Carolina. Fiscal effort is particularly low in Massachusetts. Given the strength of the state's economy, policy makers could substantially increase state education aid by increasing the state's fiscal effort to the national average. Fiscal effort is also relatively low in California and Texas, both with inadequate education systems (by the measure presented in the first column). The absence of a state income tax in Texas and Proposition 13 limits on property tax revenues in California constrain policy makers from raising fiscal effort.

PROGRESSIVITY

Baker et al. (2021) define a school funding system as progressive if it sends more revenue to school districts with high poverty (30 percent or more) than to districts with no poverty. After adjusting revenues for regional wage variation, school district size, and population density, they compare high- and no-poverty districts.

Table 5.2

Measures of Educational Adequacy and Fiscal Effort, 2019

	Adequacy	Effort
Case Study States	Percentage Difference Between Actual and Adequate Spending in High-Poverty School Districts	Total State and Local Government K–12 Spending as a Percentage of Gross State Product
California	-26%	3.0%
Massachusetts	6%	2.8%
South Carolina	-46%	3.9%
Texas	-48%	3.2%
Wisconsin	-18%	3.5%

Note: Adequate spending is the estimated amount of money needed to achieve national average NAEP test scores in the highest-poverty quintile of districts.
Source: Albert Shanker Institute and Rutgers University Graduate School of Education (2021)

Table 5.3 presents the percentage differences between per-pupil revenues in high- and zero-poverty districts; positive percentages indicate progressivity and negative percentages regressivity.

In Massachusetts, per-pupil state funding in high-poverty districts exceeds that in zero-poverty districts by more than 200 percent. In South Carolina, high-poverty districts get 5 percent more state aid per student than zero-poverty districts. South Carolina could begin to address its inadequate funding of high-poverty schools (see table 5.2, page 63) by reforming its state-aid formulas to target more aid to poor school districts. Although not shown here, South Carolina also provides inadequate funding to school districts with the smallest share of poor students. This suggests that additional funding is the only way the state can provide all its students an adequate education, but its already high fiscal effort obviously constrains South Carolina's ability to increase funding.

By providing more state aid to high-poverty school districts, California has a highly progressive system of state aid. But when combined with highly regressive local government resources, California's system is only mildly progressive. California's poorest students receive an inadequate education (see table 5.2, page 63) despite the state's overall progressive pattern of funding, which indicates that the modest (16 percent) additional funding for poor districts is insufficient. Wisconsin is similar, with state and local per-pupil revenues the same in high- and zero-poverty districts and with per-pupil spending in the highest-poverty quintile 18 percent less than the amount required for an adequate education.

Although the allocation of state aid is highly progressive in Massachusetts and Texas, overall state and local funding is mildly regressive when combined with a regressive distribution of local revenues. Despite its regressive education funding system, however, Massachusetts provides an adequate education (see table 5.2, page 63) to its poorest students. Its funding system is regressive because it does not limit per-pupil revenues (and spending) in high-wealth school districts and because referenda frequently override Proposition 2½'s property tax levy limits.

Table 5.3

Measures of Progressivity in State Aid and State-Local Revenue Distribution, 2019

	Baker et al. Progressivity Indicator	
	State Aid	State and Local Government Revenue
Case Study States	Percentage Difference in Cost-Adjusted State Aid Between 30%-Poverty and Zero-Poverty Districts	Percentage Difference in Cost-Adjusted State and Local Revenue Between 30%-Poverty and Zero-Poverty Districts
California	154%	16%
Massachusetts	208%	-16%
South Carolina	5%	6%
Texas	144%	-7%
Wisconsin	79%	0%

Note: Estimates greater than zero indicate progressive funding; less than zero, regressive funding.
Source: Albert Shanker Institute and Rutgers University Graduate School of Education. (2021)

CHAPTER 6
Recommendations

Most policy makers nationwide share the goals of improving the quality of education, funding schools equitably, and reducing burdens the property tax places on taxpayers. The policies meant to achieve these goals, however, differ widely. Thus, no single set of policy recommendations will apply in all states, and some are more relevant to some states than others.

Strong schools are good for students, communities, and taxpayers, and both the local property tax and state aid are essential ingredients for an school finance system that achieves a high-quality education, equitable funding, and fairness for taxpayers. *Source: kali9/Getty Images/E+*

USE BOTH LOCAL PROPERTY TAX REVENUE AND STATE AID TO FUND HIGH-QUALITY EDUCATION

States should rely on revenues from both a well-functioning local property tax and a state-aid system designed to finance high-quality education for all students. Both sources of revenue have weaknesses as well as strengths. History has shown that local property taxes provide more stable funding than state aid, and states should resist calls to eliminate them as a source of school funding. When structured properly, state aid can reduce fiscal disparities among school districts caused in all states by the large differences in per-pupil property tax bases.

As long as both the property tax and state aid play a significant role in school funding, no "correct" mix of these two revenue sources exists. Massachusetts and Texas are the two case study states that rely most heavily on the property tax to fund public education. However, as shown in table 5.2, they have very different educational outcomes. Texas has the largest percentage gap between per-pupil spending in high-poverty school districts and the spending needed to meet a national standard of educational adequacy. In contrast, Massachusetts, whose students perform very well on the NAEP exams, is among the states with the smallest gap.

When structured properly, state aid can reduce fiscal disparities among school districts caused in all states by the large differences in per-pupil property tax bases.

Heavy reliance on state funding comes with risks. In California, the post-*Serrano* shift away from the local property tax resulted in reduced education spending and declines in student academic achievement as measured by state test scores. Revenues from individual and corporate income taxes and from sales taxes are much more sensitive to business cycles than are revenues from property taxes. Because state education aid is a significant part of total state government spending, declines in state revenue during recessions generally result in cuts in state aid. For example, in South Carolina, which replaced property tax revenues with state sales tax revenues, the Great Recession led to cuts in per-pupil spending (adjusted for inflation) of nearly 25 percent between 2008 and 2012.

IMPROVE EQUITY AND EFFICIENCY IN PROPERTY TAX SYSTEMS

States should improve their property tax systems, because making the property tax more equitable and efficient is likely to increase its acceptance as an important component in the financing of public education. We recommend the following reforms:

Use circuit breaker programs to target property tax relief to taxpayers with high tax bills relative to income

Circuit breakers efficiently offer tax relief to homeowners most likely to face unaffordable property tax bills (usually defined as property tax liabilities above a certain percentage of income). Circuit breakers should be available to all households facing high property tax burdens, regardless of age. Income limits and maximum credits should be high enough to bring meaningful tax relief.

As the Wisconsin and Texas cases make clear, property tax relief from tax rate reductions is highly inefficient in assisting taxpayers who most need tax relief. Rate reductions spread tax cuts among all property owners, including businesses and out-of-state owners of vacation homes.

Avoid overly restrictive assessment and property tax levy limits and relax or repeal restrictive state-imposed property tax limits

Nearly all states impose limits on property taxes. Some limits protect taxpayers from rapid changes in property tax bills, but limits also generally restrict local control of school districts and often have unintended consequences. Restrictions on assessment growth are particularly pernicious because they target tax relief to owners of properties that are gaining value and away from properties with limited growth. Because of assessment limits, property tax bills often vary substantially among owners of similarly valued homes, as clearly demonstrated in California. By restricting growth in property tax revenues, levy limits often create or perpetuate funding inequities. They are a blunt instrument that, for example, prohibits school districts from responding to rising costs due to changes in enrollment. In Wisconsin, spending inequities that existed in the mid-1990s were more or less set in stone by strict revenue limits.

Because of California's strict limit on growth in assessed values, similar homes in California, as in this neighborhood near Santa Clarita, can face vastly different tax bills. *Source: halbergman/ Getty Images/E+*

Improve the quality of property tax assessments and consider implementing more frequent property assessments

A well-functioning property tax assessment system is important to ensure both the horizontal and the vertical equity of the property tax. Infrequent assessments and inaccurate assessments of neighborhood quality have been shown to generate regressive property assessments under which relatively low-valued properties are assessed at a higher fraction of market value than higher-valued properties. More frequent reassessments and better-trained assessors will enhance the equity of the property tax.

DISTRIBUTE STATE AID FAIRLY

States should allocate state aid to local school districts in a manner that ensures that all students receive a high-quality education. To achieve this goal, state-aid formulas should fulfill the following requirements:

Set appropriate academic standards and fund students' ability to meet them

NAEP test scores and the analysis by Baker et al. (2021) of adequacy demonstrate wide differences in student achievement among states. Although undoubtedly many factors account for these large differences, low educational standards play an important role in some states. Raising state academic standards and increasing efforts to achieve them requires states to commit additional resources to K–12 education. In some states, increasing fiscal effort by state and local governments is feasible. States already exerting strong fiscal effort may have to turn to the federal government for additional financial assistance.

Use foundation formulas that account for cost and fiscal capacity differences among school districts

The minimum amount of money needed to achieve any given academic standard varies by school district. These costs depend on the socioeconomic composition of students in each district, the size of the school district, and other factors beyond the control of local school boards. As explained in chapter 3, foundation formulas fill the gap between a foundation level of per-pupil spending and the property tax revenue a school district can raise at a state-mandated millage rate. Critically, each school district's foundation level should reflect the true costs of an adequate education.

Acknowledge the higher costs of educating low-income students

Recognizing that it costs more to educate low-income students tends to make state aid highly progressive, meaning that more funding per pupil flows to high-poverty districts than to low-poverty districts. In practice, many state formulas use arbitrary student

States should design their state aid systems to ensure that all students in each school district receive a high-quality education. *Source: kali9/Getty Images/E+*

poverty weights that in most cases are much lower than evidence suggests they should be.

Adjust funding formulas to reflect inflation and changes in fiscal capacity

General price inflation increases the cost of education every year, and foundation levels must be adjusted annually to reflect price increases. Failure to do so has two consequences. First, unless local school districts increase property tax revenues as prices rise, revenue will be insufficient to provide all students an adequate education. Second, as illustrated by Texas, if property values are rising and the state-mandated tax rate remains fixed, state foundation aid will decline and the share of education funding from the property tax will increase.

General price inflation increases the cost of education every year, and foundation levels must be adjusted annually to reflect price increases.

In South Carolina, the Index of Taxpaying Ability measures school district fiscal capacities. But because the index was not changed to reflect the exemption of property taxes on owner-occupied homes mandated by Act 388, fiscal capacity has been inflated and state aid reduced for school districts with a high concentration of owner-occupied housing.

EXPAND RAINY-DAY FUNDS TO PREVENT FUTURE CUTS IN STATE AID

Rainy-day funds are budget reserve funds for use when revenues fall. State aid to schools is a major budget item for most state governments. States rely heavily on income and sales taxes, which vary a great deal over business cycles, and fall during recessions. To prevent cuts in state school aid or to reduce the severity of those cuts during recessions, state governments should use revenue surpluses generated during economic booms to build up their rainy-day funds and resist the impulse to cut taxes during booms.

INVEST FEDERAL FUNDS IN LOW-INCOME STATES

The federal government should make additional funding available to low-income states unable to raise sufficient funds to provide their students an adequate education. Title I provides school districts additional resources for educating children from economically disadvantaged families. Congress should consider either increasing the current level of Title I funding or establishing a new federal grant program of financial incentives for low-spending states to increase their ongoing investments in public K–12 education.

PROVIDE ADDITIONAL FEDERAL FUNDS TO ADDRESS PANDEMIC-RELATED LEARNING LOSSES

Learning loss has been widespread during the COVID-19 pandemic, particularly for students of color, English-language learners, and disabled students. The federal government sent unprecedented funding to school districts in response, but those funds expire in 2024. The negative effects of the pandemic on student learning are unlikely to be completely mitigated by 2024. Thus, Congress should make available additional federal aid to address ongoing pandemic-related learning loss.

References

Abbeville County School District v. State, 410 S.C. 619, 767 S.E.2d 157 (S.C. 2014).

Abbeville County School District v. State, 515 S.E.2d 535 (S.C. 1999).

Adcox, Seanna. 2019. "SC Does Not Plan to Change How the State Pays for K–12 Schools in 2020." *Post and Courier*, October 29.

Albert Shanker Institute and Rutgers University Graduate School of Education. 2021. The School Finance Indicators Database. https://www.schoolfinancedata.org/

Allen, Delia B. 2018. "From Briggs v. Elliott to Abbeville v. South Carolina: A Historical Legal Analysis of School Funding Litigation in South Carolina." Ph.D. diss., University of Georgia.

Anderson, John E. 2020. "Effects of Act 388 on School Budgets." In *A Deep Dive on South Carolina's Property Tax: Complex, Inequitable, and Uncompetitive*, vol. 2, project manager Daphne Kenyon. Cambridge, MA: Lincoln Institute of Land Policy.

Badger, Emily, and Quoctrung Bui. 2022. "The Extraordinary Wealth Created by the Pandemic Housing Market." *New York Times*, May 1.

Baker, Bruce, Matthew Di Carlo, Kayla Reist, and Mark Weber. 2021. *The Adequacy and Fairness of State School Finance Systems*, School Year 2018–2019, 4th ed. Albert Shanker Institute and Rutgers University Graduate School of Education, December.

Ballotpedia. n.d. "California Proposition 15, Tax on Commercial and Industrial Properties for Education and Local Government Funding Initiative." Accessed June 25, 2022. https://ballotpedia.org/California_Proposition_15,_Tax_on_Commercial_and_Industrial_Properties_for_Education_and_Local_Government_Funding_Initiative_(2020)

Board of Governors of the U.S. Federal Reserve System. 2022. "Households; Owners' Equity in Real Estate, Level (OEHRENWBSHNO)." FRED, Federal Reserve Bank of St. Louis. Updated June 9. https://fred.stlouisfed.org/series/OEHRENWBSHNO

Bowman, John H., Daphne A. Kenyon, Adam Langley, and Bethany P. Paquin. 2009. *Property Tax Circuit Breakers: Fair and Cost-Effective Relief for Taxpayers*. Policy Focus Report. Cambridge, MA: Lincoln Institute of Land Policy.

Brunner, Eric J., and Jon Sonstelie. 2006. "California's School Finance Reform: An Experiment in Fiscal Federalism." In *The Tiebout Model at Fifty: Essays in Public Economics in Honor of Wallace Oates*, ed. William A. Fischel. Cambridge, MA: Lincoln Institute of Land Policy.

California Department of Education. 2021. "Local Control Funding Formula Overview." November 18. https://www.cde.ca.gov/fg/aa/lc/lcffoverview.asp

California Secretary of State. 2020. "Statement of Vote: General Election November 3, 2020." https://elections.cdn.sos.ca.gov/sov/2020-general/sov/complete-sov.pdf

Case, Karl E., Jane Malme, and Ronald Rakow. n.d. "Successful Property Tax Reform in Massachusetts." Online course. Module 1. Cambridge, MA: Lincoln Institute of Land Policy. Accessed June 2, 2022. https://www.lincolninst.edu/courses-events/courses/successful-property-tax-reform-case-massachusetts

Chernick, Howard, David Copeland, and David Merriman. 2021. "The Impact of Work from Home on Commercial Property Values and the Property Tax in U.S. Cities." Policy brief. (November). Washington, DC: Institute of Tax and Economic Policy. https://itep.sfo2.digitaloceanspaces.com/2021101_PropertyTaxReport.pdf

Chester, Mitchell. 2014. "Building on 20 Years of Massachusetts Education Reform." Massachusetts Department of Elementary and Secondary Education. www.doe.mass.edu/commissioner/BuildingOnReform.pdf

Coleman, James S., Ernest Q. Campbell, Carol J. Hobson, James McPartland, Alexander M. Mood, Frederic D. Weinfeld, and Robert L. York. 1966. "Equality of Educational Opportunity." Washington, DC: U.S. Government Printing Office.

Costrell, Robert M. 2006. "Massachusetts' *Hancock* Case and the Adequacy Doctrine." Conference Paper. Rappaport Institute for Greater Boston, Kennedy School of Government, Harvard University.

Dachelet, Karole. 2019. "50-State Comparison: K–12 Funding (archive)," Denver, CO: Education Commission of the States. (August). https://www.ecs.org/50-state-comparison-k-12-funding

Delaware Department of Education. 2020. "Governor Carney, Secretary Bunting Announce One-Time Enrollment Funding for Schools." Office of the Governor (December 24). https://news.delaware.gov/2020/12/24/governor-carney-secretary-bunting-announce-one-time-enrollment-funding-for-schools/

Downes, Thomas A., and Kieran M. Killeen. 2014. "So Slow to Change: The Limited Growth of Nontax Revenues in Public Education Finance, 1991–2010." *Education Finance and Policy* 9(4) (Fall): 567–599.

Downes, Thomas A., and David Schoeman. 1998. "School Finance Reform and Private School Enrollment: Evidence from California." *Journal of Urban Economics* 43(3) (May): 418–443.

Downes, Thomas A., and Leanna Stiefel. 2015. "Measuring Equity and Adequacy in School Finance." In *Handbook of Research in Education Finance and Policy*, 2nd edition, ed. Helen F. Ladd and Margaret E. Goertz, 244–259. New York: Routledge.

Duncombe, William D., Phuong Nguyen-Hoang, and John Yinger. 2015. "Measurement of Cost Differentials." In *Handbook of Research in Education Finance and Policy*, 2nd edition, ed. Helen F. Ladd and Margaret E. Goertz, 260–278. New York: Routledge.

Duncombe, William D., and John Yinger. 2005. "How Much More Does a Disadvantaged Student Cost?" *Economics of Education Review* 24(5) (Oct.): 513–532.

———. 2007. "Does School District Consolidation Cut Costs?" *Education Finance and Policy* 2(4) (Fall): 341–375.

EdBuild. 2022. "FundEd: National Poverty Maps—Poverty." http://funded.edbuild.org/national#poverty

Edgewood Independent School District v. Kirby et al., 777 S.W.2d 391 (1989).

Evans, William N., Robert M. Schwab, and Kathryn L. Wagner. 2019. "The Great Recession and Public Education." *Education Finance and Policy* 14(2) (Spring): 298–326.

Farmer, Liz. 2021. "Making a Good Tax Better." *Land Lines*. (January).

Feldstein, Martin S. 1975. "Wealth Neutrality and Local Choice in Public Education," *American Economic Review* 65(1) (March): 75–89.

Fensterwald, John. 2021. "Projected K–12 Drops in Enrollment Pose Immediate Upheaval and Decade-Long Challenge." EdSource. (October 18). https://edsource.org/2021/projected-K–12-drops-in-enrollment-pose-immediate-upheaval-and-decade-long-challenge/662531

Fischel, William A. 1989. "Did *Serrano* Cause Proposition 13?" *National Tax Journal* 42(4) (December): 465–474.

———. 2001. *The Homevoter Hypothesis.* Cambridge, MA: Harvard University Press.

Fischer, Adrienne, Chris Duncombe, and Eric Syverson. 2021. *50-State Comparison: K–12 and Special Education Funding.* Denver, CO: Education Commission of the States. (October 13). https://www.ecs.org/50-state-comparison-k-12-and-special-education-funding

Fisher, Ronald C. 2016. *State and Local Public Finance.* London: Routledge.

———. 2021. "Property Taxes: What Everybody Needs to Know." Working paper No. WP21RF1. Cambridge, MA: Lincoln Institute of Land Policy. (September). https://www.lincolninst.edu/publications/working-papers/property-taxes/

Gallup. 2019. "Trust in Government." https://news.gallup.com/poll/5392/trust-government.aspx

Goldhaber, Dan, Thomas Kane, Andrew McEachin, Emily Morton, Tyler Patterson, and Douglas O. Staiger. 2022. *The Consequences of Remote and Hybrid Instruction During the Pandemic*. Research Report. Cambridge, MA: Center for Education Policy Research, Harvard University. (May).

Hancock v. Driscoll, 443 Mass. 428 (2005).

Hanushek, Eric A. 2003. "The Failure of Input-Based Schooling Policies." *Economic Journal* 113(1) (February): 64–98.

Haveman, Mark. 2020. "Time to Reassess the State Property Tax." Minnesota Center for Fiscal Excellence. https://www.fiscalexcellence.org/policy/property-taxes/generaltax.html

Hedges, Larry Vernon, Richard D. Laine, and Rob Greenwald. 1994. "Does Money Matter? A Meta-Analysis of Studies of the Effects of Differential School Inputs on Student Outcomes." *Educational Researcher* 23(3) (April): 5–14.

Hussar, William J., and Tabitha M. Bailey. 2020. *Projections of Education Statistics to 2028*, 47th ed., NCES 2020-024. Washington, DC: National Center for Education Statistics.

Hyman, Joshua. 2017. "Does Money Matter in the Long Run? Effects of School Spending on Educational Attainment." *American Economic Journal: Economic Policy* 9(4) (November): 256–280.

Imazeki, Jennifer, and Andrew Reschovsky. 2004. "School Finance Reform in Texas: A Never-Ending Story?" In *Helping Children Left Behind: State Aid and the Pursuit of Educational Equity*, ed. John Yinger, 251–281. Cambridge, MA: MIT Press.

Jackson, C. Kirabo. 2018. "Does School Spending Matter? The New Literature on an Old Question." Working paper No. 25368. Cambridge, MA: National Bureau of Economic Research. (December).

Kava, Russ. 2021. "School District Revenue Limits and Referenda." Informational paper 26. Wisconsin Legislative Fiscal Bureau. (January). https://docs.legis.wisconsin.gov/misc/lfb/informational_papers/january_2021/0026_school_district_revenue_limits_and_referenda_informational_paper_26.pdf

Kava, Russ, and Emma Drilias. 2019. "Local Government Revenue and Expenditure Limits." Informational paper 12. Wisconsin Legislative Fiscal Bureau. (January). https://docs.legis.wisconsin.gov/misc/lfb/informational_papers/january_2019/0012_local_government_expenditure_and_revenue_limits_informational_paper_12.pdf

Kenyon, Daphne A. 2007. *The Property Tax–School Funding Dilemma*. Policy Focus Report. Cambridge, MA: Lincoln Institute of Land Policy. (December).

Kenyon, Daphne A., and Semida Munteanu. 2021. "Effects of Reducing the Role of the Local Property Tax in Funding K–12 Education." Working paper No. WP21DK1. Cambridge, MA: Lincoln Institute of Land Policy. (November).

Kenyon, Daphne A., Semida Munteanu, and Bethany Paquin. 2023. "School Funding Litigation." Working paper No. WP23DK1 Cambridge, MA: Lincoln Institute of Land Policy.

Korman, Hailly T.N., Bonnie O'Keefe, and Matt Repka. 2020. "Missing in the Margins 2020: Estimating the Scale of the COVID-19 Attendance Crisis." Bellwether Education. (October 21). https://bellwethereducation.org/publication/missing-margins-estimating-scale-covid-19-attendance-crisis#How%20did%20you%20estimate%201-3%20million%20missing%20students

Langley, Adam. 2018. "Improving the Property Tax by Expanding Options for Monthly Payments." Working paper WP18AL1. Cambridge, MA: Lincoln Institute of Land Policy. (January).

Langley, Adam, and Joan Youngman. 2021. *Property Tax Relief for Homeowners*. Policy Focus Report. Cambridge, MA: Lincoln Institute of Land Policy. https://www.lincolninst.edu/publications/policy-focus-reports/property-tax-relief-homeowners

Lav, Iris J., and Michael Leachman. 2018. "State Limits on Property Taxes Hamstring Local Services and Should Be Relaxed or Repealed." Washington, DC: Center on Budget and Policy Priorities. (July 18). https://www.cbpp.org/research/state-budget-and-tax/state-limits-on-property-taxes-hamstring-local-services-and-should-be

Lee, Soomi. 2020. "Parcel Tax in California Cities, Counties, Special Districts: New Findings from New Data Sources." *Cityscape* 22(2): 63–73.

Lincoln Institute of Land Policy and George Washington Institute of Public Policy (GWIPP). 2022. "Significant Features of the Property Tax." https://www.lincolninst.edu/research-data/data-toolkits/significant-features-property-tax

Lincoln Institute of Land Policy. 2022. "State-by-State Property Tax at a Glance." https://www.lincolninst.edu/research-data/data-toolkits/significant-features-property-tax/state-state-property-tax-glance/property-tax-data-visualization

———. n.d. "Property Tax 101: The Mechanics." Video. Accessed June 25, 2022. https://www.youtube.com/watch?v=DwrzjA9Qe3A

Martin, Naomi. 2021. "Low-Income Students Are Receiving 'Game-Changer' Student Opportunity Act Funding." *Boston Globe*, July 17.

Massachusetts Business Alliance for Education. 1991. *Every Child a Winner!* Boston: Massachusetts Business Alliance for Education. mbae.org/every-child-a-winner

McDuffy v. Secretary of the Executive Office of Education, 415 Mass. 545, 615 N.E.2d 516 (1993).

Minnesota Rural Education Association. 2021. "Pandemic Enrollment Loss Support Aid Helps Districts Who Lost Students." (October 14). https://www.mreavoice.org/pandemic-enrollment-loss-support-aid-helps-districts-who-lost-students

Morath v. Texas Taxpayer & Student Fairness Coalition, 490 S.W.3d 826 (2016).

Mullins, Daniel, and Kimberly Cox. 1995. *Tax and Expenditure Limits on Local Governments*, M-194. Washington, DC: Advisory Commission on Intergovernmental Relations.

NAEP (National Assessment of Education Progress). 2021. *The Nation's Report Card.* Washington, DC: National Center for Education Statistics.

NASBO (National Association of State Budget Officers). 2021. *The Fiscal Survey of States, Fall 2021.* Washington, DC: NASBO.

NCES (National Center for Education Statistics). 2020. "Percentage of Related Children Ages 5 to 17 Living in Poverty." In *Digest of Education Statistics*, chap. 1, table 102.45. https://nces.ed.gov/programs/digest/d20/tables/dt20_102.45.asp

———. 2021a. "Elementary and Secondary Education." In *Digest of Education Statistics*, chap. 2, tables 219.46, 235.10, and 236.65. https://nces.ed.gov/programs/digest/2021menu_tables.asp

———. 2021b. *National Public Education Financial Survey Data.* https://nces.ed.gov/ccd/files.asp. (Click through the three drop-down menus.)

———. 2021c. "New Data Reveal Public School Enrollment Decreased 3 Percent in 2020–21 School Year." (July 26). https://ies.ed.gov/blogs/nces/post/new-data-reveal-public-school-enrollment-decreased-3-percent-in-2020-21-school-year

Neeley v. West Orange-Cove Consolidated Independent School District et al., 176 S.W.3d 746 (2005).

Nelson, Ashlyn Aiko, and Beth Gazley. 2014. "The Rise of School-Supporting Nonprofits." *Education Finance and Policy* 9(4) (Fall): 541–566.

Nordlinger v. Hahn, 505 U.S. 1, 112 S. Ct. 2326, 120 L.Ed.2d 1 (1992).

Odden, Allan R., and Lawrence O. Picus. 2020. *School Finance: A Policy Perspective*. 6th ed. New York: McGraw-Hill.

Oliff, Phil, and Michael Leachman. 2011. "New School Year Brings Steep Cuts in State Funding for Schools." Washington, DC: Center on Budget and Policy Priorities. (October 7).

Ouellette, John. 2018. "Two Decades into Education Reform Effort, Commission Calls for Substantial Changes to Funding Formula." *Municipal Advocate* 29(2): 16–21. https://41g41s33vxdd2vc05w415s1e-wpengine.netdna-ssl.com/wp-content/uploads/2018/07/advocate_v29n2_foundation_budget_review_commsn-1.pdf

Paquin, Bethany P. 2015a. "Chronicle of the 161-Year History of State-Imposed Property Tax Limitations." Working paper No. WP15BP1. Cambridge, MA: Lincoln Institute of Land Policy. (April). https://www.lincolninst.edu/sites/default/files/pubfiles/paquin-wp15bp1.pdf

———. 2015b. "State-Imposed Property Tax Limitations: Trends and Outlook." *Tax Notes*. August 24. https://www.taxnotes.com/tax-notes-state/property-taxation/state-imposed-property-tax-limitations-trends-and-outlook/2015/08/24/b9r2

Picus, Lawrence O., Margaret E. Goertz, and Allan R. Odden. 2015. "Intergovernmental Aid Formulas and Case Studies," In *Handbook of Research in Education Finance and Policy*, 2nd ed., ed. Helen F. Ladd and Margaret E. Goertz, 279–296. New York: Routledge.

Ramani, Arjun, and Nicholas Bloom. 2021. "The Donut Effect of Covid-19 on Cities." Working paper No. 28876. Cambridge, MA: National Bureau of Economic Research. (May). https://www.nber.org/system/files/working_papers/w28876/w28876.pdf

Reschovsky, Andrew. 2010. "A Critical Review of Property Tax Relief in Wisconsin." *Tax Notes*, February 8. https://www.taxnotes.com/tax-notes-state/property-taxation/critical-review-property-tax-relief-wisconsin/2010/02/08/9xkn

Reschovsky, Andrew, and Jennifer Imazeki. 1998. "The Development of School Finance Formulas to Guarantee the Provision of Adequate Education to Low-Income Students." In *Developments in School Finance: 1997*, ed. William J. Fowler Jr., 121–148. NCES Publication no. 98-212. Washington, DC: National Center for Education Statistics, U.S. Department of Education.

Rueben, Kim S., Richard C. Auxier, and Tracy Gordon. 2020. "California's K–12 Education Needs." Brief. Washington, DC: Urban Institute. (July 20). https://www.urban.org/research/publication/californias-k-12-education-needs

Salazar, John, and Ellen W. Saltzman. 2013. "Act 388 and School Funding in Beaufort County, South Carolina." *Publications* 8. https://tigerprints.clemson.edu/sti_pubs/8

Saltzman, Ellen W., and Holley H. Ulbrich. 2012. "Act 388 Revisited." Clemson University's Jim Self Center on the Future. https://my.lwv.org/sites/default/files/act_388_revisited_november_2012_.pdf

San Antonio Independent School District v. Rodriguez, 411 U.S. 1, 93 S.Ct. 1278, 36 L.Ed.2d 16 (1973).

Saving, Jason L. 2018. "Texas Property Taxes Soar as Homeowners Confront Rising Values." *Southwest Economy* (Q3) 7–11.

SchoolFunding.Info. 2021. "South Carolina." New York: Center for Educational Equity, Teachers College, Columbia University. https://www.schoolfunding.info/litigation-map/south-carolina/#1485211082372-7e6ae017-5d39

Serrano v. Priest, 5 Cal.3d 584, 487 P.2d 1241 (1971) (*Serrano I*).

Serrano v. Priest, 18 Cal.3d 728, 5557 P.2d 929 (1976) (*Serrano II*).

Serrano v. Priest, 226 Cal. Rptr. 584 (Court of Appeal, 2d District) (1986) (*Serrano III*).

Shores, Kenneth, and Matthew P. Steinberg. 2019. "The Great Recession, Fiscal Federalism and the Consequences for Cross-District Spending Inequality." *Journal of Education Finance* 45(2) (Fall): 123–148.

Sjoquist, David L., and Andrew V. Stephenson. 2010. "An Analysis of Alternative Revenue Sources for Local Governments." In *Municipal Revenues and Land Policies*, ed. Gregory K. Ingram and Yu-Hung Hong. Cambridge, MA: Lincoln Institute of Land Policy.

Slade, David. 2020. "Development Impact Fees Can Now Be Used for School Construction, South Carolina Districts Are Learning." *Post and Courier*, December 16.

Sonstelie, Jon. 2014. "California's Parcel Tax." Working paper No. WP14JS1. Cambridge, MA: Lincoln Institute of Land Policy. https://www.lincolninst.edu/sites/default/files/pubfiles/sonstelie-wp14js1.pdf

Sonstelie, Jon, Eric J. Brunner, and Kenneth Ardon. 2000. *For Better or for Worse? School Finance Reform in California*. San Francisco: Public Policy Institute of California. (February).

Sorensen, Lucy, Youngsung Kim, and Moontae Hwang. 2021. "The Distributional Effects of Property Tax Constraints on School Districts." *National Tax Journal* 74(3) (September): 621–654.

South Carolina Revenue and Fiscal Affairs Office. 2022. "Property Tax Reimbursement Projections, Homestead Exemption Fund (Tier III)." https://rfa.sc.gov/sites/default/files/2022-02/40%20-%20Homestead%20Exemption%20Fund%20Tier%20III%20-FY%2023%2002.15.22%20Table_0.pdf

Taylor, Lori L., and William J. Fowler. 2006. *A Comparable Wage Approach to Geographic Cost Adjustment*. Washington, DC: National Center for Education Statistics U.S. Department of Education.

Texas Education Agency. 2021a. *2019–20 Texas Academic Performance Reports.* https://rptsvr1.tea.texas.gov/perfreport/tapr/2020/index.html

———. 2021b. "Average Daily Attendance and Wealth per Average Daily Attendance." https://tea.texas.gov/finance-and-grants/state-funding/state-funding-reports-and-data/average-daily-attendance-and-wealth-per-average-daily-attendance

———. 2021c. *PEIMS District Financial Actual Reports.* https://tea.texas.gov/finance-and-grants/state-funding/state-funding-reports-and-data/peims-financial-standard-reports

Texas Legislative Budget Board. 2020. *Fiscal Size-Up, 2020–2021 Biennium.* Fig. 150. Austin: Legislative Budget Board. (May).

Texas Office of the Governor. 2021. "State Leadership Announces Funding for Texas School Systems to Support In-Person Instruction." (March 4). https://gov.texas.gov/news/post/state-leadership-announces-funding-for-texas-school-systems-to-support-in-person-instruction

Thomas, Stephen B., and Billy Don Walker. 1982. "Texas Public School Education," *Journal of Education Finance* 8(2) (Fall): 223–281.

Town of Sudbury v. Commissioner of Corporations & Taxation, 366 Mass. 558, 321 N.E.2d 641 (1974).

Ullrich, Laura Dawson. 2013. "Act 388: Its Impacts on South Carolina Schools and Communities." Paper presented at the annual meeting of the International Association of Assessing Officers, Grand Rapids, MI (August 26).

U.S. Census Bureau. 1972, 1977–1991. *Finances of Public School Systems.* Washington, DC: U.S. Government Printing Office.

———. 1992–2020. *Annual Survey of School System Finance* (F33). https://www.census.gov/programs-surveys/school-finances.html.

———. 2010–2019. "Median Real Estate Taxes Paid" (B25103) and "Median Household Income" (B19013), American Community Survey, 1-Year Estimates, 2010 to 2019. Washington, DC: U.S. Government Printing Office

———. 2019. *2017 Census of Governments—Organization.* Table 9: Public School Systems by Type of Organization and State. https://www.census.gov/data/tables/2017/econ/gus/2017-governments.html

———. 2022. *2020 Public Elementary-Secondary Education Finance Data.* https://www2.census.gov/programs-surveys/school-finances/tables/2020/secondary-education-finance/elsec20_sumtables.xls

U.S. Department of Education. 2002. *The No Child Left Behind Act of 2001: The Public Law print of PL 107-110.* https://files.eric.ed.gov/fulltext/ED556108.pdf

Urban-Brookings Tax Policy Center. n.d. "State and Local Finance Data." Accessed June 25, 2022. https://state-local-finance-data.taxpolicycenter.org/pages.cfm

Urban Institute. 2022. "South Carolina." State Fiscal Briefs. May.

Wen, Christine, Yuanshuo Xu, Yunji Kim, and Mildred E. Warner. 2018. "Starving Counties, Squeezing Cities: Tax and Expenditure Limits in the US." *Journal of Economic Policy Reform* 23(2): 101–119.

Youngman, Joan. 2016. *A Good Tax.* Cambridge, MA: Lincoln Institute of Land Policy.

Acknowledgments

The authors are grateful to the experts who made helpful comments on this report, including Carrie Conaway, former chief strategy and research officer, Massachusetts Department of Elementary and Secondary Education and senior lecturer, Harvard University Graduate School of Education; Thomas Downes, professor of economics, Tufts University; Michael Griffith, senior researcher and policy analyst, Learning Policy Institute; Kieran Killeen, professor of economics, University of Vermont; Therese McGuire, professor of strategy, Kellogg School of Management, Northwestern University; Lawrence O. Picus, Richard T. and Mary Catherine Cooper chair in public school administration, University of Southern California Rossier School of Education; Kim Rueben, Sol Price Fellow and director of the state and local finance initiative, Urban-Brookings Tax Policy Center; Lori Taylor, professor and head of public service and administration department, the Bush School of Government and Public Service, Texas A&M University; Daniel Thatcher, senior fellow, Education Finance Policy, National Conference of State Legislatures; and Laura Ullrich, senior regional economist at the Charlotte branch of the Federal Reserve Bank of Richmond.

We also thank Alannah Shute, Ph.D. student at the University of Tennessee, for her very helpful research assistance and our colleagues Anthony Flint, Adam Langley, Joan Youngman, and Sydney Zelinka for their advice and support. We extend special thanks to Allison Ehrich Bernstein, Kevin Clarke, Amy Finch, and Emily McKeigue for their expert editorial contributions.

ABOUT THE AUTHORS

Daphne A. Kenyon, principal, D. A. Kenyon and Associates, served as resident fellow in tax policy at the Lincoln Institute of Land Policy, where she coauthored several reports, including *The Property Tax–School Funding Dilemma*, *Payments in Lieu of Taxes* (with Adam Langley), and *Rethinking Property Tax Incentives for Business* (with Adam Langley and Bethany Paquin), and was coeditor (with Gregory Ingram) of *Education, Land, and Location*. Kenyon's prior positions include president of the Josiah Bartlett Center for Public Policy, professor and chair of the Economics Department at Simmons College, senior economist with the U.S. Department of the Treasury and the Urban Institute, and assistant professor at Dartmouth College. She is the 2022–2023 president of the National Tax Association. Kenyon served on the New Hampshire State Board of Education and as a New Hampshire representative to the Education Commission of the States. Kenyon earned her B.A. in economics from Michigan State University and her M.A. and Ph.D. in economics from the University of Michigan.

Bethany Paquin is a senior research analyst in the department of valuation and taxation at the Lincoln Institute of Land Policy. She is director of the State-by-State Property Tax at a Glance data toolkit. Her research has contributed to Lincoln Institute reports on school finance and payments in lieu of taxes. She has published articles on property tax limitations and is a coauthor of two Lincoln Institute Policy Focus Reports: *Property Tax Circuit Breakers: Fair and Cost-Effective Relief for Taxpayers* (with John Bowman, Daphne A. Kenyon, and Adam Langley) and *Rethinking Property Tax Incentives for Business* (with Daphne A. Kenyon and Adam Langley). She previously worked as a research assistant for the public finance consulting firm D. A. Kenyon and Associates. She earned a B.A. in political science from Grove City College.

Andrew Reschovsky is a professor emeritus of public affairs and applied economics at the University of Wisconsin–Madison. He has published widely on topics related to state and local government finance. He has testified to state legislatures on education funding and served as an expert witness for the plaintiffs in a case that successfully challenged the constitutionality of the Texas school finance system. He has also served as an advisor to the Organization of Economic Cooperation and Development in Paris and the South African Financial and Fiscal Commission. In 2014, he coedited (with Daphne Kenyon) a special issue of *Education Finance and Policy* on the property tax and the funding of K–12 education. He has published numerous papers on funding public education in the United States in journals including the *National Tax Journal*, *Public Finance Review*, and *Peabody Journal of Education*. In 2011, he was awarded the Steven D. Gold award by the Association of Public Policy Analysis and Management in recognition of his contributions to state and local fiscal policy. He earned a Ph.D. in economics from the University of Pennsylvania.